Dear Mama, You Matter

Dear Mama, You Matter

Honest talk about the transition to motherhood

Amanda Hardy, PhD, LMHC

Foreword by Alyssa D. Berlin, PsyD
Illustrations by Holly Norian

Edited by Dallas Woodburn and Courtney Kimsey
Cover and interior design: Holly Norian, Fancy Fox
Illustrations © Holly Norian, Fancy Fox

ISBN: 979-8-62592-125-1 (paperback)

Available in paperback and ebook

Printed in the United States of America

Disclaimer: The information provided within this book is for informational and educational purposes only and does not create a therapist-client relationship. Furthermore, the information obtained from this book is not intended to assess, diagnose, or treat and medical and/or mental health disease or condition. If you have any questions about your specific health, seek the advice of your physician, nurse practitioner, physician assistant, therapist, counselor, mental health practitioner, licensed dietitian or nutritionist, or any other licensed or registered health care professional.

The Internet addresses, books, podcasts, etc. referenced in this book are offered as a resource. They are not intended in any way to be or imply an endorsement by the author, nor does the author vouch for the content of these websites for the life of this book.

To my village and my committee.
Thank you for mothering me in the midst of the mess.

Contents

Part II: You Are Enough

Part III: Connection

Part IV: When It's More Than Just Hard

Foreword

I remember that beautiful day in early June, after months of preparation, nausea, strain on my body, an exhausting multi-day labor and birth. That beautiful day. After all the hard work, sweat and tears. The first time home with baby. My husband sitting next to me. All smiles. All joy. The moment we had been picturing for so long. My first day as a mommy. What could possibly be better?

And then the vortex hit me. Fast.

With no training and a steep learning curve. I'm feeding, bathing, changing and caring for a newborn, who, by the way, primarily would communicate his needs by screaming at me, all as I am sleeping less, seeing self-care fade into my rearview mirror, and not fully understanding the new relationship dynamics in my brand new family unit. Phew!

Needless to say, it didn't take long before I felt physically and emotionally run down.

Unfortunately, this story is not unique to me. In today's lightning quick and flashy society, we tend to spend pregnancy focused more on belly pics, birth stories, labor day and baby gear, and forget about the final step. What happens after birth?

Through my nearly 15 years of practice as a pre- and postnatal psychologist, counseling thousands of new and expectant individuals and couples, I see the same story every day.

Postpartum is filled with huge changes over short periods of time. Days before having your baby, people are magically kind, giving up their seats, opening doors and smiling at you and your growing bump. But during postpartum when you do things like get on an airplane with a baby, you are more likely to get nervous stares and angry looks if your baby begins to fuss or cry. Postpartum can feel lonely and unsupported and, surprisingly, be the most difficult period of time for a new mom.

But it doesn't have to be.

Thankfully my colleague, Amanda Hardy is changing the narrative with her new book, *Dear Mama, You Matter*—a look into the situations, challenges, and stories mamas face in the often forgotten postpartum phase. This book is great for expecting mothers, first-time mothers, and mothers at any other stage. *Dear Mama, You Matter* is universal. The compassion and wisdom that Amanda is known for are bottled up for you to consume in the pages of this book.

As I read through Amanda's stories and tips, I could relate both as a mother and as a perinatal professional. In my Online Workshop, "The Afterbirth Plan for New and Expectant Couples," I seek and provide couples with the best list of resources to complement our work together. I am thrilled to add *Dear Mama, You Matter* to that list.

Amanda does a great job reinforcing the ideas we as therapists teach in a very insightful and easy read. This book is also a fantastic resource for people who can't see regular professionals or who are looking for more perspective on postpartum. Reading this book will undoubtedly enhance life for new mothers.

Amanda's goal is to make sure all mothers feel like they matter. Once you read *Dear Mama, You Matter* and its many helpful tips, you will feel uplifted and have greater appreciation for your postpartum self. Read *Dear Mama, You Matter* so you can feel prepared, excited, and ready to assume your lifelong role as a mama and make every day a beautiful day.

Alyssa D. Berlin, PsyD
Clinical Psychologist
Berlin Wellness Group

Author's Statement

This book is not a substitute for medical or therapeutic advice. Take everything shared within these pages with careful, thoughtful, and intentional consideration. I am not you and I do not know your situation. You do. You are the expert on you and your experiences and circumstances. From these pages, take what works for you and leave the rest. If you are struggling, please reach out to your family, friends, or your healthcare provider.

This book is not merely for those who gave birth and identify as a "mama." I recognize the many complex and beautiful paths to parenthood and the diverse relationship structures that each family uniquely creates. Each of these paths and experiences is valuable. While mamas are clearly a key focus of this book and referenced throughout, I also intentionally use more gender-neutral parenting terms. Whether or not you gave birth to your baby or came to parenthood by a different path, I want you to know this book is for you, too.

The focus of this book is a summation of my work in the childbirth and parenting fields. This book discusses experiences from my years of research and work with families as they transition to parenthood that are nearly universal. This means that most people will experience some or all of these things. For some, the hard stuff I speak about in these pages is more than just difficult—it's super difficult or even traumatic. For others, you may have barely registered some of these experiences as difficult—it was "not too bad" for you. I want to acknowledge that we all walk different paths, and while I hope you find some bits of relatability here, it may not be the case for you. Your story and your journey matter, even if I didn't hit on it as deeply within these pages. I see you.

Finally, I believe it's important to recognize that the place I'm speaking from is of a cisgender white woman who has worked and studied in a predominately white community with people who are more often than not also cis and identify as "mama." The stories and experiences of all parents are valuable and deserve to be told. However, I believe I am not the person to speak to all these experiences at any great depth, as they are not my expertise. I want to recognize this place from which I am speaking while also welcoming any parent, regardless of their journey, to find some solace in these pages. Regardless of whether or not you call yourself mama, daddy, or baba (or any other name), the experiences of the "default parent" have many universal truths, and that's what I'm attempting to speak to in this book. I am also learning and listening. I am a flawed human who will make mistakes. I remain open and accepting of the lessons that will come my way over the course of my life's journey.

The stories shared within are either shared with permission (pseudonyms used) or are composites of stories shared with me through research, therapy, or my life as a doula, educator, and friend.

"*The moment a child is born, the mother is also born. She never existed before. The woman existed, but the mother, never. A mother is something absolutely new.*"

Osho

Introduction

Once a baby is born, so much of the focus and energy turns toward them. After all, they are extremely dependent and needy little humans that require so much of our time. It's natural for all the books and chatter to be about those sweet and squishy little cherubs that have entered our lives. However, someone else is in the midst of this. Someone going through changes from the depths of their core to their actual physical being. That person matters, too. That person is worthy of our time and attention and a bit of our chatter. That person is you, mama. You matter. And these words are for you.

A few days before I was scheduled to submit this manuscript to my editor, an interview with the Duchess of Sussex, Meghan Markle, was released. The interview was part of the documentary *Harry & Meghan: An African Journey*. Tom Bradby from ITV asked the Duchess "Are you okay?" in regards to her journey of becoming a royal and a new mom. Her response immediately went viral. She said, "Thank you for asking because not many people have asked if I'm okay." The response went viral, in my opinion, because new mothers everywhere wholeheartedly relate to it. And the response became reassurance that this book is important. Mamas all over the world need to be reminded that they matter and to be asked, "Are you okay?" This book is for anyone who has ever felt like Meghan.

I've been working with families as they transition to parenthood for over a decade, and it's often assumed that I must love babies to do this work. "No," I usually reply. It's not that I dislike babies. I mean, bring on those cute squishy bellies and that sweet smell! It's just that my love is more for the mamas. I do the work I do for the mamas. **Because the more we love on the mamas, the more they can love on their babies.** Loving on those babies is one of the most powerful things we can do. We can change the world by raising our children to know they are deeply loved and that they matter. The best way I know to do this is by showing mamas that they are also deeply loved and that they matter.

When you were expecting your baby, you undoubtedly heard people talk about how hard it is to have a baby. Often this is explained with discussions of hormones and sleep deprivation. This isn't wrong, of course—both of those play a role in the challenges of our earliest days of parenthood, but I think they provide an incomplete picture. Our socio-emotional experiences provide some of the biggest personal challenges during our transition to parenthood. Shining light on these areas—arguably more within our control than sleep and hormones—can help us better understand why it's so hard and perhaps set a course for tackling some of those challenges.

Giving birth can be a challenging experience. It's also the easiest part of parenting. I'm not the first to say this. I remember feeling so well-prepared for my birth and then afterwards thinking, "Oh god, I have to raise this human now."

This writing is a walk through some of those "oh god" moments many of us experience as new parents. Whether we're a parent for the first time or a parent again. Whether we're a birthing parent or an adoptive parent, there are universal challenges we all face—from the influence of cultural norms and narratives to the deeply personal and intimate realities of our daily lives. In this book, we'll:

- Explore the influence of birth practices in America. How do these experiences influence us, and most of all, how might they impact our early days of parenting?

- Dive into the fourth trimester and matrescence and address the ways in which we need to mourn some potential losses as we become parents.

- Address some common myths with powerful undercurrents that influence how we think about what mothering should look and feel like.

- Examine the ways we can connect and reconnect to ourselves and our community to improve our overall well-being.

- While this book is not about experiences with perinatal mood and anxiety disorders, we will talk about how to identify those and some of the ways to treat them.

There is great (and necessary) content about what to expect during pregnancy and birth, about the developmental milestones of our children (i.e., baby's first year), and even on postpartum depression or anxiety (i.e., when it's more than baseline hard stuff). However, few books seem to *focus on the mama* and the personal experiences of transitioning to parenthood. I feel this is a significant gap and one that is quite reflective of our cultural norms about motherhood. In this book, I focus on what I call the "baseline hard stuff" surrounding this transition. I blend research and professional experience with personal stories and a nice dash of humor to make this book authentic and accessible. What I call "honest talk" in my title is ultimately aimed at normalizing the challenges of our transition to parenthood. My goal is to acknowledge that hard is really normal. And by demystifying this hard stuff, I am hopeful you'll find reassurance for your journey and perhaps connectedness with others as well.

I invite you to join me in this honest conversation, and I hope some of these words will feel like a healing and soothing salve for your mama heart. I also hope some tidbits I share here provide a subtle, yet profound, easing of your transition to parenthood. I imagine you reading this with a sweet baby nuzzled close to your heart (hopefully snoozing peacefully). And as I imagine you there, in your nursing tank, sweats, covered in spit-up, questioning when you last showered, I hope you find yourself feeling more normal and confident about your own motherhood journey. I have compiled these topics as a series of short essays meant to be easy to digest and light. Within each essay, I share tips and tricks along with stories "from the trenches" and resources to offer practical techniques. As with anything you read, take what works for you and leave the rest.

Background

ON BECOMING A MOTHER[1]

One of the first experiences most people have on their journey to motherhood is the maternity care system. While this book does not focus on childbirth or this system in great detail, acknowledging the role this journey plays is beneficial. Regardless of where or how you gave birth, your experiences within this system affected you.

This section is a critique of the medical system not the providers who work within it. However, it is essential to note that the United States is having a maternity care crisis. Americans spend more money on healthcare than any other nation and have some of the worst outcomes, especially for people of color. Like all institutions and systems that were established long ago, the issues are multifaceted and complex. I have studied childbirth experiences for the past decade in both academic and activist contexts, I have been

---

[1] I want to acknowledge that all paths to parenthood are relevant here. Becoming a parent through adoption or surrogacy or any other means also impacts us. Your unique experiences matter too. I see you.

with families as a doula during birth, and I work as a mental health provider specializing in the perinatal period. I've also worked with a number of local, national, and international organizations all with the aim of improving outcomes for families when it comes to pregnancy, birth, and postpartum transition. These experiences have given me a unique perspective on this crisis.

My dissertation study was an exploration of the history of birth in America through a feminist lens. My guiding question was *how did we get here (maternity care crisis) and what does it mean for moms, babies, and families?* Nearly a decade later, I'm still asking that question. While this book isn't dedicated to the first part of that question, it certainly is focused on the second one. For me, these two questions are linked, and that's why I want to share this brief background addressing how we got here.

Working in this field beyond my own childbearing has led people to ask me why I care so much. In the briefest of summaries, I care about birth because every mother and family deserves access to start well. Birth matters. Approaching pregnancy and birth in a holistic manner is best practice and preventive medicine, in my opinion. I want every person to have what I call a mountain top moment after giving birth—to feel that euphoric high you get from having summited a mountain. It's a feeling like you can conquer the world! I think that's a pretty great place for everyone to start on their parenthood journey.

I want to be very clear about my intent with this section. The following is critical in nature. I call into question and challenge the systemic and structural layers surrounding our maternity care climate and culture. It is important to note that this is NOT an attack on the individuals who work within these systems. It's a common and expected response to think, "Hey lady! That doctor saved my life and my baby's life" or "My baby would have died if it wasn't for the hospital." There is no denying that hospitals save lives, and that is a very good thing. Additionally, the people who work within these systems are usually very caring and competent individuals. While critiquing a system we can also recognize the gains or benefits from these systems. Much like one might argue that we have gained convenience from the invention of automobiles, it also comes with other unintended (or unable to be seen at the time) consequences. This is what I want to highlight—we've gained much, but some of these gains have brought potential costs. We cannot ignore these costs, as they impact our lives.

For me, it's important to take in this whole picture and shine a light on what's often left out or even actively suppressed in our dominant narrative surrounding birth. Why is this important to the postpartum experience? How we feel about our birth experiences cannot be underestimated in shaping our earliest days of parenting. How we experience the maternity care culture can and does affect us. The critical question I am forced to ask—and ultimately, my challenge to the maternity care system—is **are we building up our mothers to feel strong, capable, and confident through our interactions with them?**

SOCIAL CONSTRUCTION

"We don't see things as they are, we see them as we are."

Anaïs Nin

A social construct is a shared idea that we, as a social group, collectively create and assign meaning to. The concept of social construction suggests that social groups collectively create meaning. Simply put, it's all a made-up construction, from the stories we tell ourselves to why we're all still sending each other fruitcakes at Christmas. We assign (construct) meaning to everything— from what trees are used for (shade, oxygen, beauty, or toilet paper) to what time of day is appropriate to call someone on the phone (not at "dinner time" or after 9 p.m.).

Social Construct (n): an idea that has been created and accepted by the people in a society.

If we are to understand how we got here, we have to understand the power of social construction. We create roles, norms, rules, systems, and cultures around these ideas. One of the best and, I think, easiest ways to understand social construction and its impact on our lives is to ask yourself, "Why do I do that?"

Naturally, we socially construct our world because we're social beings. We have spoken (explicit) and unspoken (implicit) rules about all manner of things. These shared meanings and stories are often referred to as "cultural narratives." Princesses get rescued from the dragon by sword-wielding knights on horses and they live happily ever after, right? You may also think about this as our ideas about how things are *supposed* to go. These cultural narratives and social constructions are incredibly powerful. If you are interacting with

ALL HANDS ON DECK

A quick example of a social construct. In my house, I want the whole family involved in the dinnertime experience. Menu planning, shopping, cooking, participating in dinner chatter, and (heck yes) cleaning up. That's an **idea.** A **concept** I want to **build** into the **structure** of our home life. I can make official rules about this, but, most likely, we'll just start doing certain things. We'll talk about it like it's our **norm,** that it's everyone's **role** to participate. Through repetition, this will just become **what we do.** I can socially construct that idea. Years from now when my children are grown and visit me, what do you think they'll do? Most likely, they'll jump right in and join me in dinner activities. They'll probably do this in other areas of their life too with friends and partners because I **created the narrative** about what we do around mealtime.

This is one example of something I've constructed in my home. There are other narratives that you might value over this one. Perhaps it's participating in regular religious or spiritual rituals, or exercise and being outdoors. Maybe it's something as simple as a bedtime or goodbye routine. The point here is we can choose what we want to create/construct based on our own personal values.

people in the world—from your immediate family members to the grocery store cashier—you are both participating in and co-creating our world. You are being influenced by and also influencing (creating and shaping), through your participation, our social world all the time.

Now that we've gotten through that quick primer on social construction, what does it have to do with our birth and parenting experiences? Barbara Katz Rothman published a piece in the 1977 summer issue of the *American College of Nurse-Midwives* journal titled, "The Social Construction of Birth." What Katz Rothman points out with the title of her publication is that our maternity care system, like all social systems, is a construction. She notes that this system is one in which pregnant and birthing people can feel isolated and disconnected from their own experiences, all of which can lead to poor mental and physical health outcomes before, during, and after birth as well as challenges during the transition to parenthood. One of the key arguments for this finding is the notion of "turf" or "who is in charge" of birth, a birthing body, and the birth space. My own research has replicated similar findings in the voices of my participants.

The French philosopher Michel Foucault coined the term "medical gaze" in his 1963 book *The Birth of the Clinic*. The term describes the way that medical establishment separates a person's identity from their body (not in a literal sense). He argued that this separation is dehumanizing. We're not a person giving birth; instead, we become our condition. From my own research, I hear women reporting feeling like a number rather than a person. For example, rather than "Amanda, giving birth in room 1054," I become "the prime (first birth) in room 1054 at 4 cm with no heplock." Where's the human being in that description?

The simple fact is childbirth has been socially constructed as a medical condition requiring medical attention and hospitalization. Plenty of people are quick to point out how necessary and life-saving this has been. That's okay. We're not addressing it with this book. What's important to realize is that the idea of pregnancy as a medical condition shapes how we think about a person when they are pregnant and when birthing.

We must acknowledge that the hospital is the territory of medical providers. They set the rules. They are in charge. There is an inherent power dynamic at play there. My own research and experiences with families during this time has highlighted this power inequity again and again. As a result of this dynamic, women hear (and internalize) two clear messages (and these messages matter):

1. You (and your baby) are inherently at risk.

2. If you're to be safe, you need to relinquish control to someone else.

One of the most common phrases I hear when listening to birth stories is "they allowed me" or "they wouldn't allow me," which demonstrates this power dynamic. If we consider that a pregnant or birthing person is not inherently unwell, sick, or in danger and rather that the condition of pregnancy is a normal healthy function of the body, our entire idea around *how* we give birth and why we do *what we do* shifts. This is the medical gaze. Viewing pregnancy and birth through this lens shapes what we think and how we respond as a result.

Research and feedback from parents indicates that this medical gaze values only one outcome: a healthy baby. You've all heard it, "...at least you have a healthy baby." Unpacking that notion could be an entire book in itself. Here's how this narrative (and the underlying assumptions that come with it) can affect a new parent.

My baby is healthy.

- How I'm feeling doesn't matter.

- How I was treated doesn't matter.
- What I went through doesn't matter.
- Parental health and well-being doesn't matter.
- I must sacrifice myself for the health of my baby.

This idea that the baby is all that matters is deeply depersonalizing. It can separate the birthing person from their body. Anthropologist Robbie Davis-Floyd has written extensively on this subject. Feeling like merely a vessel for the baby, not a living, breathing, thinking, feeling, human being who also matters can have profound psychological consequences. I'm confident many of you, my dear readers, can relate to that feeling on a deeply personal level.

Too often we see new parents going home with a *healthy baby*, and they aren't feeling holistically healthy themselves. This situation is a big problem. A healthy baby matters, and no one would agree with that statement more than the parents, but healthy parents also matter. It is entirely possible that **we can prioritize both of these outcomes.** Healthy babies *and* healthy families should be the goal on birth days and after. Feeling that you matter and you are much more than a baby incubator is a big deal. The medical gaze can often fail to take this more holistic view, which can be detrimental.

The question my research has led me to ask (and why I'm including this brief background section in this book) is this: **is our current maternity care system set up to ensure we all start well?**

After more than a decade of research and work in this field, I have concluded that how you gave birth isn't what matters—whether you gave birth vaginally or via Cesarean, unmedicated or with an epidural, with midwives or OBs, at home, the hospital or a birth center—**what truly matters is how you are made to feel during your birth.**

A mother who feels that she was belittled, coerced, or (yes) even forced to do something during her birthing experience has been done a disservice. As a result, she may very well experience emotional turmoil (or trauma) that a woman who felt supported, nurtured, and centered during her birth would less likely grapple with. No, not everyone gets their own version of the "perfect" birth. That's not what I'm talking about here. What I want to make abundantly and overwhelmingly clear is that **there is always room for every single birthing person to be treated with the utmost dignity, respect, and reverence for the life-altering experiences they are going through.**

> "Birth is not only about making babies. Birth is also about making mothers—strong, competent, capable mothers who trust themselves and know their inner strength."
>
> Barbra Katz Rothman

In my years working with birthing families, I have seen and heard many, many things. Things I'd label as "bad" and plenty I'd label as "good." No two births are the same, that's for sure. I have been with families as they have faced unimaginable decisions. I've sat with couples while they have made decisions to change course and alter plans. Even seemingly simple decisions have emotional challenges.

There is one thing I've never seen: I have never, not once, seen weakness from a mother. Never. Birth, whatever course it takes, is powerful and all-consuming. It's beautiful and hard all at the same time. Mothers rise to the occasion every single time. That's what I see when I've been invited into someone's birth space as a doula or am gifted the opportunity to hear birth stories as a therapist or a researcher. Women rise to the occasion. I am continually in awe and

CHANGE IS HAPPENING ALL THE TIME

A generation ago, fathers were relegated to waiting rooms (with their cigars at the ready), and now we couldn't imagine our partners not being present with us in the delivery room. That idea shifted and we shifted with it. Now, if I asked you why you had your partner with you during labor and delivery, you'd probably look at me a little sideways and say, "Well, that's just what you do." This transition means that, as we (socially) shift our gaze from the narrow medical one (which often focuses on physical health outcomes exclusively) to one with a more holistic well-being (which considers the overall health of the whole system), we can only imagine what might be "just what you do" for the next generation.

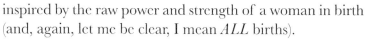

inspired by the raw power and strength of a woman in birth (and, again, let me be clear, I mean *ALL* births).

However, what I see isn't what I hear reported. Too many women have internalized negative feelings from their births, and I am concerned about where these feelings stem from, the deeply personal (long-term) impact they have, and how we might address them.

My research has shown there is an unacknowledged and unintended consequence of our current system: a feeling of self-doubt. I often hear some form of the phrase, "I really doubted myself" when someone is telling their birth story. Others say different things that clearly point to this notion: "I didn't think I could do it" or "in my weakness."

If we feel that our bodies (our very nature) are insufficient or even "broken" (another word I hear women use frequently), this undoubtedly influences how we face future challenges (ahem, motherhood) that demand us to pull from some internal reservoir of innate guiding knowledge, skills, or abilities.

We cannot discount the cumulative impact of these feelings on our psyche. "I couldn't go into labor on my own," "failed induction," "I didn't make enough milk," etc. These experiences and the deeply personal ways in which we interpret and internalize them impact how we'll face the next thing that comes our way. And, as parents, there is always a new challenge coming at us.

In short, an optimally functioning maternity care system should take this full picture—how a person feels—into account. Ensuring that families feel valued, confident, and capable after their time in the maternity care system and not merely living and breathing (though we, of course, want that too) can and should be prioritized.

Our perceptions and expectations shape how we interact with the world and then mix with our interpretations of our actual lived experiences. How we experience the maternity care culture can and does impact us. **We don't experience our births in isolation from the rest of our lives.** In fact, it's quite the opposite. Our birth experiences are deeply personal and, simply put, influence how we think and feel about ourselves. In turn, this affects how we think about our abilities as we enter into our parenting journey. If you exit the maternity care system feeling somehow broken, belittled, or incapable and then you face an inevitable parenting challenge, those feelings are with you. **Our experiences matter. You matter. You are more than a vessel.**

It's necessary to reflect on our maternity care experiences to understand that they're relevant to how we're feeling now. This background is an invitation to personally reflect on the context of your own unique experiences in birth.

"The most dangerous stories we make up are the narratives that diminish our inherent worthiness. We must reclaim the truth about our lovability."

Brené Brown

RECLAIM YOUR NARRATIVE

I worked with a client whose vulnerability mixed with self-doubt during her birth had a strong impact on her. She described feeling like she had to perform, yet she didn't know how or what to do. She said she felt like everyone was just watching her, expecting her to be able to do something. She felt scared.

This mama carried this feeling of fear, self-doubt, and uncertainty with her and was in a sort of hyper-research mode about anything and everything to do with her child, desperate for confirmation and validation that she was "doing it right."

During one session, I asked if I could tell her what I heard when she told me her birth story. I told her I heard strength in her vulnerability. "You were doing it. You didn't need help. You were capable and powerful, and they trusted you to get the job done. And you did do it. You. Just you." She told me that she had never thought about it like that. I could tell she was letting this perspective sink in. She was entertaining the idea that she was an amazing rock star (as I saw her).

We had a few more sessions. She was lighter each time. One day, as we again revisited her birth story, she said, **"I did do that. I'm pretty awesome!"**

*"I knew it would be hard,
but I didn't know it would be this kind of hard."*

Every new parent ever

PART I
Hard Is Normal

Dear Mama,

It's hard. Hard is so normal. And you can do hard things.

You've heard this before. In fact, I'm guessing when you were pregnant or planning to become pregnant you got pretty annoyed with people reminding you that it's hard, as if maybe these people didn't know you'd already been told. Like they were warning you again and again. Or maybe there was even some fear and frustration that people were telling you this— again and again—meant that they didn't think you could do hard things.

Oh mama, I know you can do hard things.

I also know this isn't like any other hard thing you've ever done before.

You can do it. You will do it.

And it's hard.

One of the reasons it's hard is because we can't actually prepare for it. No matter how many times we were oh-so-gently and kindly reminded that this job was going to be tough, we just can't know until we're really in the thick of it. I remember waking up all those times in the night (let's be honest, it was probably only two to three) to go to the bathroom at the end of pregnancy and thinking, "oh this is just preparing me for getting up in the night with a baby." Ha! NOT EVEN CLOSE. Of course, I don't just mean that sleep deprivation is hard. I mean, it is, but it's only one piece of this hard-as-hell pie you're eating right now.

Another big reason it's hard, perhaps the most misunderstood and unacknowledged reason, is new parents are in the process of becoming something new! The magazines and the dominant cultural narrative love to talk about when we're going "back." Getting our body back! Getting our life back. Back to our old selves. This idea implies that we're just ourselves but with a baby in tow. As if a baby just fits into this carved out little corner of our lives and everything goes on pretty much as normal. This idea is bullshit. It's an absolutely absurd notion, and I think it's actually hurting us. Imagine how differently you'd think about your postpartum and transition to parenthood if our cultural story was about reinvention and redefinition of ourselves as we transitioned to parenthood, rather than going back. No one wants to think the person they've become—the only person they've ever been—is gone. And that's not an accurate way to think about it *either. Of course you will still be you. You'll just be a reimagined version of you.*

Becoming is a verb. We are constantly in the process of becoming. We are always changing, reinventing, adapting, and becoming something new. Often these changes go unnoticed. They are subtle, in the day to day. It's not until we think back to our 16-year-old selves do we really realize just how much we've changed. The difference in the postpartum is the messaging around NOT changing. On the going back and staying the same. As if change is bad.

I don't say this to be dismissive, but the truth is you're not going back. You're not that you anymore. You're not. And that's okay. That's exciting and new and scary and everything in between.

If we can meet this—struggle, between being me and becoming—head on and turn into it with awareness, we can dissolve a lot of the tension around this issue. Instead of feeling that you're failing or falling short on the "going back" to your old self, assess those messages from a more informed place and reduce the feelings of fear, shame, or guilt. You're less likely to get caught in the undercurrent of those stories if you know it's coming and have the tools to handle the transition to motherhood.

So don't buy into that message of going "back."
Instead approach this transition with curiosity and
even excitement as you continue on life's journey of
becoming. Consider this time as an opportunity to
invent and reinvent this newer, parent version of you.
Doing so can help make hard things less hard and
reduces points of tension, strain, and self-judgment.

With love,
Amanda

"[Sail your ship] into the straits of motherhood. You are always alone and never alone in that fragile and tensile craft."

Jane Taylor

Sail Your Ship

L ife is like sailing the seas. We're each in our own boat. Our first boats are often somewhat rickety and uncertain, but as we move through life, we upgrade and make improvements. We also become more and more confident at sailing. When and if we choose to couple, we often join our little boats or come into port and upgrade to a bigger and (ideally) more cohesive ship.

As you can imagine, and I'm sure you've felt, navigating the seas while lashed to someone else's boat that's navigated in a totally different way than yours is challenging. Does that not sound like the basis of every argument you've ever had in a relationship? Sometimes seas rage. Sometimes we capsize. Sometimes we change course.

Here's what I like about this metaphor for families: **the goal is sailing the ship.** It's as simple and as hard as that. To accomplish this goal, we need to recognize the needs of the boat to meet that goal.

- We need to understand how this ship runs. What are the jobs to keep us afloat and on course? Who does those jobs?

- Navigating the course means we have to set a course in the first place. Where do we want our boat to go? What are our goals?

- We learn to read the wind and the water. How to weather storms and batten down the hatches. We monitor our inventory and re-evaluate constantly. We communicate (then we communicate again).

- Sometimes, we dock and wait for a season or a storm. Sometimes, storms catch us by surprise. Sometimes, it's smooth sailing and beautiful seas.

Becoming a family means entering uncharted waters. Often, our boat is bigger with more bells and whistles and maintenance requirements. It's a daunting task to sail a boat across the sea. It can be scary and overwhelming out in the wide-open ocean. It is also a breathtaking and exciting adventure. Success at this task—our life's work—requires many skills. Most of which we haven't honed yet because we haven't needed them. Learning while doing (and maybe before we're ready) is often required.

This is family life. Big waves that toss us around, and even scare us, and gentle little waves that lull us as we travel. Ups and downs. Highs and lows. Gentle and rough. Scary and beautiful. Funny and frightening.

"Welcome to the end of being alone inside your mind
You're tethered to another and you're worried all the time
You always knew the melody but you never heard it rhyme

...

The first things that she took from me were selfishness and sleep
She broke a thousand heirlooms I was never meant to keep
She filled my life with color, canceled plans, and trashed my car
But none of that was ever who we are."

Brandi Carlile, "The Mother"

The Fourth Trimester

Pediatrician Harvey Karp is credited with coining the phrase "the fourth trimester" in his 2001 book *The Happiest Baby on the Block*. Sarah Ockwell-Smith has also published extensively on this subject. Her signature 2012 article, "The Fourth Trimester—AKA Why Your Newborn Baby is Only Happy in Your Arms," beautifully articulates the significance of this period in development. In 2017, Kimberly Ann Johnson wrote *The Fourth Trimester: A Postpartum Guide to Healing Your Body, Balancing Your Emotions and Restoring Your Vitality*. In short, the term to describe this period has caught on, and many scholars and professionals have provided outstanding commentary on the matter. I highly recommend checking out works by these authors and acknowledge that it is their work, among others, that I'm summarizing here.

The fourth trimester is such an important concept to understand and the key time period that this book focuses on. What exactly is the fourth trimester? It is the first few months of your baby's life. If we're getting technical, it's the first three months. However, I always like to say three to four months because babies vary, and from a developmental standpoint, I think it stretches past three and a bit into four. The exact date of the fourth trimester ending is neither here nor there. What's important is understanding the concepts associated with it and why it matters.

The word "trimester" is used to highlight the continuation of the dependency a baby has on the mother. During pregnancy, the baby is 100 percent dependent on the mother. Guess what? That's the theme of the fourth trimester: baby is still pretty (ahem, extremely) dependent on mama for those first couple months.

The human infant is the most dependent of all mammals. They literally need a caregiver to survive unlike those baby giraffes that are up and walking within hours of birth. It's actually important that we frame some of this understanding in terms of survival because it's helpful for us to

DEFAULT PARENT

The person who the baby has identified as most essential to their survival. The way in which babies identify this person is an evolutionary survival mechanism. Often, this person serves as primary caregiver, especially in those early days. The default parent is likely the main source of food, comfort, and other care tasks. The default parent is often the mother. However, please note that a default parent is identified (by the baby) in families that formed via adoption and of course non-birthing parents can and certainly do fill this role for a baby, too. It's about survival for a baby, not the person. In some instances, a baby's preference between their parental caregivers will be indistinct. In other cases, their preferences are quite apparent and even intense. What's noteworthy is that these preferences and "defaulting" behavior is about survival.

recognize where our tiny humans are coming from. All the demands they place on us are based on a survival instinct.

So, when we think of the fourth trimester, we think about a very high needs mammal. The neediest. And it's just as awful as it sounds (I'm kidding, kind of). Understanding this dependency can help us meet our babies' needs with greater empathy and understanding (through the fog and exhaustion).

So what are the needs of a human infant:

1. Nourishment: no shocker there, we need food
2. Sleep: our bodies do important work during sleep
3. Cleanliness: obviously, hygiene
4. To be held: touch is a human need
5. Warm and responsive caregiving: our demeanor does matter

Many of the baby books focus on physical developmental milestones, but, in my opinion, fail to highlight the importance of these most basic needs. I think numbers 1 through 3 above are pretty obvious and few would question them. The last two that are usually a sticky point or the ones we don't think or talk about as often.

Research has long demonstrated the impact of touch on human development. We know that in extreme cases lack of touch can result in failure to thrive and even death. This is scary and certainly extreme, but it emphasizes just how important touch is. Studies have also demonstrated that a warm and loving response to our babies' requests (ahem, cries) can positively impact their cognitive development. Simply responding in a gentle voice to our child's cries or with a smile on our face promotes neurological development. How we respond to our children's requests is associated with attachment development, which is all about developing trust (more about this in Chapter 17: A Primer on Attachment).

Now that we have a basic understanding of these needs, what the heck does this have to do with the first few months of a baby's life? Well, everything. **Those first few months can be summarized in one word: transition.** Both the parents and the new baby experience transition. Baby is transitioning from their womb world to the outside world and there are many changes. In the womb, baby's every need was immediately met. One might even argue that they never had a need because they were always fed, clean, warm, and held. The womb is dark, quiet, and the perfect temperature. Being in the outside world means they must ask for their needs to be met (via their one and only method: crying). The outside world means they must also wait for their needs to be met. The world can be cold and loud and isolating. That's scary. Truly, it's scary for them. It may be helpful to think of a baby's developing brain like a circuit board. Except this circuit board has only

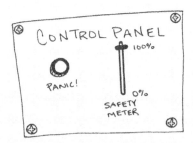

Sometimes, the word 'manipulation' is used when talking about babies crying. I have a little beef with the use of that word when we're talking about babies or even young children. Manipulation is a complex cognitive concept that a newborn is simply not capable of. Period. What they are capable of is using every single one of their few resources to communicate their needs (i.e., crying).

two features (for now). Their brains have—in essence—two tracks: track 1. I'm safe, this is okay, and track 2. I'm not safe; this is not okay.

Babies have all their senses on all the time. Of course, we all use our senses all the time to interact with the world (see Chapter 6: Sensitivity). However, babies don't yet have the sophisticated means to decode and interpret the data they constantly receive. Therefore, they can be extremely sensitive. Hunger, a dirty diaper, the light and sounds in a room, temperatures can send babies down track 2. Any situation that isn't a Goldilocks "just right" situation can trigger the survival ("danger") alarm bells to go off. The baby simply does not yet have the cognitive capacity to process information beyond survival mode. Those neurons are firing, yes, and they're laying down the groundwork to expand that circuit board to be able to process more complex information, but it's just the basics when they are first born.

When we apply this knowledge about what a baby's womb world was like and why the outside world—even with very loving parents—might be scary for them, we can meet their needs in a different way. And, heck, even be preemptive about addressing these needs. Recognizing this can help ease some of the challenges of this transition phase. It also helps us

Neuroscience research shows us that a baby's central, motor, and cardiac regulations are all calmed when being carried or held. Other studies have suggested that babies become familiar with the canter in their mother's walk, the rhythm of her voice, her scent, and her heartbeat. The mother is attached to that safe womb world and often the safety of food and comfort in the outside world (especially if breastfeeding). When we understand why a baby feels this way, we can appreciate the baby's need to be close to their source of safety.

answer the question, "Why is baby only happy when I'm holding them?" Because their survival instinct tells them it's safer, plain and simple. (And, yes, totally exhausting.)

There are two key things that I want to focus on beyond our basic understanding of some of the science that affect us as parents:

1. For the mama or default parent, being the baby's primary caregiver can be overwhelming and exhausting.

2. For the partner or non-default parent, it can be frustrating and even hurtful to feel like your baby doesn't want you, seek you for comfort, or that you can't be helpful to your partner. This circumstance can be a heavy burden.

Talking about these new roles as parents and partners can be one of the most powerful things we can do to weather the challenges of the fourth trimester.

A tired mama "stuck" at home with a brand new baby hasn't showered in a solid few days, is covered in dried breast milk and spit up, has been trapped on the couch all day under a sleeping baby, and has to pee. She wants nothing more than to pass that baby off to dad when he walks through the door at the end of the day. Baby is not so keen to this idea. Who is this person with a different smell, a different heartbeat, a different walk holding me? Danger! "No thank you," says the baby. Poor mama is just ready for a break. "C'mon baby, this is your other parent. They love you, too. Let them hold you and comfort you." Dad is eager to see the baby and wants to bond and, not to mention, give Mom that break she's been waiting on all day.

You can see how this extremely common scenario can be frustrating and disappointing for both parents. One wants the help; the other wants to help. The baby has other ideas. Non-default parents can feel really defeated at these responses. "My baby doesn't like me" or "I'm not a good parent" or "We'll never bond" aren't uncommon thoughts and feelings. They are hard, sad, and scary feelings, but you're not alone in them. Mama (or the default parent) can get increasingly frustrated and exhausted by this scene. Being the only one who seems to be able to comfort the baby feels endless, exhausting, and draining, which can lead to

When planning for postpartum, proactively preparing for this idea—that baby is only happy in mama's arms—is essential. Here are a couple thoughts to consider as you plan.

Awareness: Be aware that it's a normal thing (hard, but normal).

Recognition: Recognize what's happening and why. Transitions take time.

Validation: This one is key—both parents (and the baby) have feelings about how the transition is going. Make space in your conversations for all those feelings to exist.

Planning: What is the best course of action for us? How can we address some of our family's concerns with unique feelings and circumstances?

Implementation: Put your plan into practice. Remember, the first thing you try might not always be the winner. Experiment.

feeling defeated and depleted.

Recognizing the common and inevitable challenges you may likely face in the fourth trimester allows both parents the opportunity to talk openly about their experiences and plan for how to best address them. Looking at this period as an extension of the pregnancy and seeing mom and baby as one (mama-baby unit) may help us frame what we need to do. The cord may be cut, but baby isn't so sure if that was a good idea. Looking at mama (or the default parent) and baby as one entity can be helpful.

The best way to meet everyone's needs is unique to each family and each situation. Here are a few ideas to help you have discussions with your co-parent or partner about navigating the fourth trimester:

- Recognize that what baby is doing is normal and temporary. The fourth trimester—like all stages—doesn't last forever (see Chapter 15: Life is Messy, Get Dirty).

- Re-examine the distribution of "chores" around the house and ask how to keep mom comfy (bring snacks, always bring snacks).

- Discuss how that break will happen. Maybe dad and baby go for a nice walk outside because mama isn't going to be able to get that quick nap or enjoy that shower if she can hear baby crying and knows she can offer comfort (for the record, mothers' brains also change during pregnancy and birth to be hyper-aware of their infants' crying).

- If nothing else, being able to understand and validate each other's feelings about the struggles can go a long way! We're on the same team here. It's hard for both of us in some very similar and unique ways. Feeling secure in that can mean the world.

TIPS FOR PARTNERS

Support can take many forms, but here are a few tips for partners to support the mother-baby unit:

Ask. Yes, it's that simple. Ask how things have been going and then just listen. Don't listen to problem solve. Then ask if there are problems that could be solved and work collectively to brainstorm solutions.

Bring snacks. Keep the water bottle full and nursing nest stocked with go-to, easy snacks. Many mamas report feeling a bit trapped under a nursing or sleeping baby in those early days. Helping to keep her well hydrated and fed is a great way to offer support.

Entertainment. Perhaps a movie night would feel good, a new book, magazines, maybe play cards, or have a stimulating conversation. Ask what would feel like a mental break from the tasks of caring for the baby all day.

Encouraging words. Hearing your partner say you're doing a great job and you're appreciated goes a long way. Trust me, she probably thinks she's not doing it right, so a dose of respect, gratitude, and encouragement will not be misguided.

Let her sleep. I know that getting ready and doing what you've got to do is hard with a baby in tow. Believe me, I know! However, giving her 20 to 30 minutes of sleep while you hangout and chill with the baby while you're getting ready (or whenever you're offering this sleep time) might be the highlight of her day. I'm serious, it really might be the highlight—that's life with a newborn, so see if you can't find a way to let her catch some zzzs.

"Motherhood transforms us. It's not that we become different people or we lose ourselves. It's that we discover feelings, impulses, thoughts, and wishes within ourselves that we likely never would have encountered had we not become mothers."

Molly Millwood

Matrescence

One of the hardest realities of motherhood is that it changes you. When and how deeply this reality hits a new mother varies, as most things do. However, during my tenure in this field, I have found that it is universal. **You are not the same person you were before you had a baby.**

I know that seems so simple. And I know you're probably reading that thinking, "Well, duh!" But I cannot tell you how profound this transition is. I'm not talking about a title or a role; I'm talking about one's identity.

We have a word for this transition, which is helpful, but we don't yet have the social constructs and cultural narratives in place that truly capture the significance of it, let alone actually support it. The word for this transition is **matrescence.** It was originally coined by medical anthropologist Dr. Dana Raphel in 1973. However, the word didn't really hit the mainstream until the fall of 2018 when Dr. Alexandra Sacks gave a TED Talk titled, "A new way to think about the transition to motherhood," in which she focused on the power of language and the need for a word to help us understand this time of transition. Dr. Sacks along with Dr. Catherine Birndorf, both reproductive psychiatrists, published a book on this topic in early 2019 called, *What No One Tells You: A Guide to Your Emotions from Pregnancy to Motherhood*. No surprise, Dr. Sacks's work with families during their transition to parenthood is quite similar to my own and the conclusion of her TED Talk echoes the arc of my book: it's all about connection (but more on that later).

Most of us are quite familiar with adolescence. That time when our hormones surge, and we trudge somewhat uncertain through puberty to emerge on the other side an alleged adult. Child development theorist Erik Erikson's 1963 theory of psychosocial development suggests that the task of adolescence is identity development. In essence, what we all know and have experienced in some capacity is the idea that we're all trying to "figure out who we are" during adolescence.

Apply this same concept to motherhood—trying to figure out who you are (again). But this idea is far more than simply figuring out your *role* as a mother. A role might be understood as our costumes or uniforms we wear in a given context. Something we can take on or off. I "wear" my role as a professor, which comes with various jargon, attitudes, demeanor, and, yes, even attire. One's identity is much more than a role. It's to the core. We can't take it on or off or step in and out of it. It is us.

What I mean here and what I want to make clear is becoming a mother redefines *you*. You're not the same you. It's not just learning a new job. Not even close. It's a second adolescence. Except this time you're also helping this other new and extremely dependent little human thrive and grow. Easy, right?

I told you this was a hard reality. What I just said might seem extreme or intense. It is and it isn't. It is a big deal!

It's also a totally normal thing. A hard thing, but a normal thing.

What this looks like and how it "hits" us varies. Here's what I hear so many mamas say:

- "I don't even know who I was before I had the baby."
- "I don't recognize myself."
- "I feel totally lost."
- "I feel like the person I was is gone."

These are common phrases and experiences. These are normal experiences. However, just because something is normal or common doesn't mean it's not hard. Please don't hear this language as a dismissal. For some, these experiences are really scary and overwhelming. Some days can feel like storms that capsize our little boat or merely some bumpy waves other times. These winds of change might be welcome and exciting for some and terrifying for others. How we face these inevitable storms is wholly unique and depends on our experiences, resources, and tools available to us. As well, there is also an inherent sense of grief and loss attached to this experience, which often goes unacknowledged (see Chapter 5: Mourning).

You've spent your whole life becoming yourself. Becoming that pre-mother person. Or maybe you're a second or third time parent and you've spent a lot of time figuring out how to navigate these waters of parenthood and now a new tiny human is throwing you off course a bit. You're a new parent whether it's for the first time or for the second, third, fourth, and so on. You've never done this exact thing with this unique tiny human before. I was one of these mamas who didn't report too many challenges with my first baby, but I felt a bit like the boat capsized after the second one came along.

Our cultural stories tell us that having a baby is just *you* and *a baby*. Like an extra little accessory. You + baby. But the baby is not an accessory. Having a baby changes your life in almost every single way. So when we ask, "When are you getting **back** to yourself? Back to your body? Back to work? Back to your hobbies and interests and style?" You may feel that something is "wrong" with you if you're not back or don't feel like going back.

- Why don't I feel like myself?
- Why do I feel lost?
- Where have I gone and why can't I get her back?

I hear these types of words from my clients at least once per week.

I share this with you because I believe understanding and naming this helps to normalize it. It also helps to change our discussions and expectations. **The moment that we can recognize, honor, and create space for this reality— that we're not going back—the more we can help ourselves and each other.**

I have often used the metaphor of a butterfly when talking about the transition to motherhood.

This can be a bit of a fuzzy line. Identity changes are developmentally normal (common and expected) as we transition to parenthood. Meaning, while it should be expected that you might not feel like yourself, how intensely you're experiencing these feelings of not being yourself can also be a sign that you're experiencing a perinatal mood or anxiety disorder (PMAD). See Chapter 27 for more information.

It seems cliché, but bear with me. When a fresh butterfly emerges from its chrysalis, it doesn't immediately begin to fly. It sits and suns itself. It dries out its brand new wings. It's just been through a big change. It was one thing, and now it's another. An entirely new thing. It's not ready to use all this new equipment. It suns for hours. Then, it will flap its wings, testing. It will do this for some time before actually taking flight.

"When she transformed into a butterfly, the caterpillar spoke not of her beauty, but of her weirdness. They wanted her to change back into what she always had been. But she had wings."

Dean Jackson

Let's take this metaphor and ask ourselves if our society asks, "How are you doing sunning those new wings, mama?" HELL NO! Instead, it's, "Hey, when are you going to be a caterpillar again doing all those caterpillar things?"

Some moms are acutely aware that they are no longer a caterpillar. They feel this deep in their souls. *I am not that thing anymore. Yet I also don't quite know what to do with this new self. These wings feel odd and confusing.* This situation can cause angst.

Some moms are trying so hard to still be a caterpillar doing all their caterpillar things (because they want to, need to, or society tells them to, or any combination thereof). For some women, that works pretty well. It's only when the wind blows and catches those wings or the rains come and soak those wings that they feel something is amiss. This can cause angst.

Some moms feel stunned by emerging from the chrysalis. They don't feel they are a caterpillar anymore, and they don't feel they are a butterfly. They feel uncertain and confused. This can cause angst.

The more we talk about these experiences—about the metamorphosis—the more new moms may be able to approach the process more prepared. **We need to stop talking about getting *back* to it and more about how the transition is going.** We need more language and spaces that honor and appreciate that an actual change is actively happening.

The first step is normalizing this issue. We've discussed that it's normal. It looks different and affects each of us differently, but the overall experience—new self-new identity-metamorphosis—is a universal experience. Just as we know the challenges and uncertainties of adolescence, we can expect the same during our transition to motherhood.

Next, we need to talk about it. We need to create spaces for these conversations. We don't shy away from conversations about teenagers and the expectations of those years. That angst is well-discussed (also, it's trivialized, but we'll address that issue another day). We also need to do away with the messages about going back. These messages often promote guilt and failure and are wrapped up in identity confusion. We would laugh at the idea of telling a 15-year-old to get back to their 8-year-old self. We owe mamas (and all parents) the same expectations. We recognize, honor, and know that life will never be what it once was. It's an absurd notion to expect to go "back," yet we say this to new mothers in nearly every conversation about new motherhood.

Share your truth. Talk about it and reject those going back ideas. While reinventing oneself is certainly challenging, we feel better when we talk about it, and we also help others through their experiences.

Finally, **give yourself grace.** Give yourself time and space. I know, *how the heck am I supposed to do that while also raising a new human?* Engage in the process. Mourn letting go of your former self. This process might be the hardest and most challenging part of this journey. You worked hard to become that self. You know what that self is capable of and how that self operates. You know what that self enjoys and needs. Here I am telling you that self is gone?

Yes and no. Let's head back to my caterpillar metaphor. Did you know that scientists have discovered that the butterfly actually retains the memory of being a caterpillar? They discovered this by training caterpillars to recognize a scent. Then, after they were butterflies, they were able to demonstrate that they remembered this scent. They remembered.

No big deal? No, a super big deal! When a caterpillar forms a chrysalis and becomes a butterfly, they aren't just growing wings inside that little shell. They are literally coming completely undone (more about this in the next chapter). They turn to utter mush, or as Dr. Marth Weiss (an author on the scent study from Georgetown University) referred to as, "caterpillar soup." Gross, I know. Not the majestic process we may have once thought it was. **Even after all that, they remember.**

If you were an extrovert, you're probably still going to be an extrovert. If you used to enjoy creating art and writing poetry, you'll still desire and value those things. There may be surprising new things that interest you. A sudden interest in gardening and homesteading—where did that come from?

So, fear not, this transformation is not always an all-or-nothing dramatic process, much like adolescence. The underlying fact is embracing these shifts and changes and newness also comes with a need to grieve.

GIVING YOURSELF GRACE

When I say give yourself grace, I mean:

- **Give yourself whatever YOU need.** (It's probably not what that lady down the street needed, and that's okay.)

- **Give yourself time.** It will take as long as it takes, and that's okay.

- **Give yourself space.** Listen and get curious about your inner self. What are you feeling? What do you need to express (internally or out loud), and are you creating spaces for the process?

Mooring (n): a permanent structure to which a vessel may be secured

Unmoored (adj): of a vessel not or no longer attached to a mooring

Feeling "Come Undone"

Becoming a parent can make some of us feel like we've come undone (remember that butterfly soup). It's a feeling like the pieces of who you know yourself to be are spread out all over the floor. Or it can feel like you're adrift at sea, having come unmoored. There's confusion and uncertainty in that place. Like so many things, this feeling can range from quite intense to mild. Whatever the degree and depth you experience this, the feeling seems to be universal among new parents.

This coming undone feeling is an extremely vulnerable place to be. Vulnerability in this context can feel like you have a diminished capacity to cope, recover, and thrive in this new role. Did I mention how messy that feels? Ick!

I'm going to say something that might be tough to hear. I think that this is a really good, and even necessary, place to be. I know, how can this feeling possibly be "good"? **This is where the growth happens.** This is where we come into our own. We stop fighting the inevitable. Yes, we've come unmoored or undone. Normal. Now what? That's when things actually get exciting (if you're a geek for personal growth and development, like me). Look around and assess the messy undone unmoored vulnerability of it all. Become aware.

We gain a better understanding of our emotional landscape when we are aware of and recognize these feelings. This provides us with better footing. When we know where we are, we can better assess how to get to where we want to go.

This is why the undoneness can actually be a very good thing. Note that I didn't say easy. When we're undone and embrace vulnerability, we have a great opportunity to determine how we want to pick up those pieces and reassemble ourselves as something new. We're in the process of becoming, and this stage is part of that process. Engaging in the experience and taking an active and aware role is most certainly to your advantage.

The more we embrace our vulnerability during this "come undone time" and adjust accordingly, the more we will thrive. **All my years of professional work and research have convinced me of this truth: there is strength in our vulnerability.**

*"It's no use going back to yesterday, because I was
a different person then."*

Lewis Carroll, Alice in Wonderland

Mourning the Loss of Pre-Parenthood You

Some people might be surprised to see a section about mourning in a book about motherhood and the postpartum journey. However, it plays a central role in our experiences. Sometimes, we're acutely aware of the role grief plays. Those waves are rocking our boat and we know it. We're paying close attention. Cautious to make sure they don't capsize us. Other times, we're less aware. Mourning may be a current just beneath the surface. It still impacts our journey and affects the direction of our boat, but it's far more subtle.

I know this one is tough, but mourning and loss is part of our journey to becoming a parent. I know that's generally not the story we like to tell ourselves or what we want to think about, especially if you've long awaited the arrival of that sweet, snuggly little baby or experienced pregnancy loss or infertility or had an otherwise difficult journey to parenthood.

It might make sense that mourning has to do with a difficult birth journey. I'm glad you may have thought that—

more validation for what I talked about in the background section (our births our connected to our other experiences). However, that's not the only type of mourning that's at play here. Mourning and grief are all about loss. And loss comes in many different forms.

In her 1969 book *On Death and Dying*, Elisabeth Kübler-Ross presented a model for grief. Commonly known as the five stages of grief: denial (and isolation), anger, bargaining, depression, and acceptance. Over time, others have expanded on these stages. Grief presents itself in many ways aside from these stages, and there is certainly some noteworthy critique of Kubler-Ross' original work. One of the tricky things about grief and mourning that most scholars will agree on is that it doesn't present itself in linear stages, and no two people grieve in the same way. It's important to note that ultimately change, in the many ways it comes to us, brings loss and can create feelings of grief. The following are common thoughts and feelings associated with each grief stage:

- Shock: I feel numb.

- Denial: This isn't happening.

- Isolation: No one understands; I just need to be alone.

- Anger: I hate everything and everyone (also expressed as rage, bitterness, or resentment).

- Bargaining: I'll make a deal with you, fate/god/universe ("if only..." thinking dominates).

- Depression/Anxiety: I don't know how I'm going to make it through this; I feel so overwhelmed.

- Acceptance: I understand that this is where I'm at and what I'm dealing with.

- Reconstruction: I can pick up the pieces and carry on.

Fifty years ago, when Kubler-Ross first published on grief, we didn't fully appreciate that it could exist outside of the context of death. We had a very narrow view, but we know better now. We know that loss comes in many forms and that grieving and mourning can be a part of our story at various stages of our lives—not only in death. We can mourn the loss of friendships, careers, and even ideas. What we now understand is that mourning is actually a pretty normal part of living. Hard, but normal.

In parenthood sometimes we grieve invisible things that others may not see or recognize, which can add a complicated layer to our grieving. It may be infertility, pregnancy loss, the birth experience you didn't have, struggles with your planned feeding decisions, a partner who returned to work too soon (or had no leave at all), no family able to support you postpartum, your maternity leave ending, and many more. I validate you if you're grieving any of these (and plenty I didn't mention). I see you in your grief. You are not alone.

What I hear parents talk about, and what the research points to, are three key areas of loss associated with the transition to parenthood:

1. Loss of freedom (I can't do what I want or need to do when or how I want.)

2. Loss of self-identity (This baby has consumed me and I don't recognize myself.)

3. Loss of social/community (I'm isolated and alone.)

Feeling a high level of freedom is linked to happiness and life satisfaction. People who feel a strong sense of freedom (personal autonomy) are more likely to report higher levels of life satisfaction and happiness. Well, guess what new parents aren't feeling? Freedom. Common descriptions of the first weeks (months) postpartum:

- "I feel trapped."
- "I can't go anywhere or do anything."
- "I am so overwhelmed."

In fact, that last one might be one of the most commonly uttered phrases from a new parent (but this conclusion is only anecdotal). When we feel this way, we can start to get foggy. It's hard to see the forest through the trees when we're feeling overwhelmed. Overwhelm can also feel like a bit of psychological paralysis. Everything gets a bit narrow and we can hyperfocus on these key survival tasks (i.e., meet the baby's needs). *Wasn't it just a second ago that I was an autonomous adult making serious decisions capable of complex thinking? Who am I and what's happening to me?*

Our babies are all consuming. Human babies are the most dependent of all mammalian babies. We've talked about this a bit earlier in this book; however, it bears repeating. They do take a significant amount, if not all, of our time and attention to survive. No, it won't be like that forever, I promise. But it's a lot, especially in those early days and weeks. Not recognizing yourself is a common feeling. It's beyond feeling like you can't engage in your normal activities. It's also feeling like your thoughts are not your own. *Can I think of anything other than the baby's schedule, please? I'm a well-accomplished adult with lots of really great thoughts in this brain and they're all blocked up with the color and consistency of my child's last bowel movement.*

People even start referring to you as "so-and-so's mom." While I know many of us feel such a great sense of joy and pride when we hear the phrase "so-and-so's mom," there are also times where it reminds us of our lack of personal identity since becoming a parent. Feeling like you are missing and you are only a baby caretaker is tough. Super tough. *Hello, I have a name. I'm a person, too.*

Feeling overwhelmed and consumed with caregiving

can be exacerbated when we're also feeling isolated, alone, or even trapped. All of this points to a major theme of this book: **we need each other.** We're not meant to raise babies alone. When we have a baby in our modern age, we are far too often isolated from our people. From our community. From our village. That's loss. So many mamas talk to me about feeling isolated. Ironically, many of them report heading to their local big box store as a means to interact with other people. Others talk about how they keep the television or a radio on all the time to give the illusion of presence of other people in their day-to-day life. After the helpful grandmothers, aunts, and others (if you were lucky enough to have them) leave and your partner returns to work, you're likely home alone all day long. Isolation is scary and yucky. Now, don't get me wrong, if you're an introvert, you can still feel this loss of community. Even though your needs for people may differ from your more extroverted friends, you are still a social being who needs people.

These feelings are hard. They speak to a deep sense of loss, which can feel confusing and consuming, but it's also normal. I believe it's very important to allow space for this grief process. Using this framework and labeling this process as one of mourning, we are being more truthful about what's happening. We're honoring the experience instead of fighting it. Or worse, applying guilt and shame to it. Some self-talk that embraces the process might sound like, "It's okay to be sad about…," or "I really miss…," or "This is different and that's hard." I talk more about this in Chapter 14: Feeling Complicated. To summarize, the idea here isn't to get rid of or stop these hard feelings, but to allow them to co-exist (perhaps even honor and welcome them) alongside other emotions. Suppressing these very real feelings often causes us more trouble and turmoil than allowing ourselves to feel them.

It's okay to feel sad or upset about the pieces of you that don't feel like you anymore and to grieve for who you were. In fact, failing to acknowledge this grieving (in its many forms) seems painful, doesn't it? It's helpful to note that you can engage in this grief process while simultaneously feeling joy in your new self and your new human. Our world has tried to convince us that to feel one thing means we can't feel another. That's bullshit! Mixed and paradoxical feelings are normal.

- Happy and in love with your child? Also, absolutely feeling like a deer in the headlights about your new life? That's normal.

- Happy that your loved one who had suffered from a chronic illness for years is no longer in pain? Also, missing them and feeling a void? Normal.

Don't try to talk yourself out of feeling whatever you're feeling. Instead, make space to honor and validate the multiple realities and complexities that make up our beautiful messy lives. One of the simplest ways to do this is by using the word "and" instead of "but" when chatting with yourself. All too often we shut down our feelings (and worse, guilt and shame ourselves) for feeling down about something.

- This might sound something like this: "I'm really struggling with how little time I feel that I have to just be by myself and relax, BUT I know I have a happy healthy baby and that's what I wanted, so I *should* feel happy."

- Instead try saying, "I'm really mourning the loss of free time I have, *and* I love my baby."

Changing how you frame your perspective allows space for both these truths to be equally valid. By allowing that idea space to be mourned, you're helping yourself grieve. It's okay to not be thrilled about all the changes and the process of becoming something new all the time. We know that grief is a non-linear process, that there's no right way to grieve, and that there's no timeline.

Sensitivity

The postpartum period is an inherently vulnerable time, which can leave us more susceptible to sensory over-stimulation and ultimately sensory overload. We are sensing beings. The information that allows us to interact in the world is sensory. Stimuli are received through our senses (touch, taste, smell, sight, sound), and we process that information in the body and send it to our brain to interpret.

This process is essential for our functioning. However, it can also be overwhelming at different times. Our bodies have filters that help shift through ALL the stimuli we are constantly exposed to that keep everything in check and, ideally, not overwhelming. In an overly simplistic definition, we have mechanisms in place that help keep the receptors from getting overloaded. An overloaded system doesn't function optimally. An overloaded system begins to operate in more of a survival mode (fight, flight, freeze, fawn). If you've felt this way, it might be the moment that you throw your hands up and just say, "I'm done. Too much!"

Everyone responds to stimuli differently. We can ex-perience changes in how we receive and process stimuli throughout our lifetime—or even over the course of the day—for many different reasons: hormonal changes, natural development and maturation, trauma, and sleep deprivation, to name a few.

You can probably see where I'm going with this. My working theory is **postpartum tips the scales toward higher sensitivity regarding these experiences.** Regardless of how you experienced processing sensory information before baby, you may be more likely to experience sensory overload in the postpartum period than you may otherwise. So, what do we do about this?

1. **Recognize the vulnerability.** Increase your awareness that sensory stimuli might be more easily flooding your system! Be gentle with yourself. Give yourself grace and understanding.

2. **Take a self-inventory.** Notice times when you experience that overloaded, full, too much feeling. Assess how stimulated you are. Understanding why you are experiencing overloaded feelings is a huge step in being able to address them.

3. **Reduce.** Awareness also offers insight to reduce stimuli. It seems simple enough, right? Well, in an ideal scenario we could control our environments to be just right. Sadly, in the real world, that "Goldilocks just right" dream scenario can be a bit harder to come by. While we certainly can't control everything, we can control some things:

   • Reduce the amount of noise in your spaces by turning off the radio and TV more. Savor the silence (or a lower hum).

   • Trust me, your child is going to be just fine without every singing and light-up toy on the market. (In fact, they might even be better off for it, but that's a different discussion).

- Opt for soft or natural lighting options in your rooms, rather than overly bright, fluorescent, or white light.

4. **Let's talk touch.** Touch might also be the most commonly noted or most obvious "too much" experience. Touch is a really tricky one to adjust in the postpartum period, especially when those babies *need* to be held often and if they are breastfeeding. Communicating with a partner about touch, sensitivity, and too much can go a long way in helping you overcome this challenging time. It's really helpful for partners to know and also look for ways to help reduce your receptors getting overloaded too fast too often.

These ideas are to help you get started. There are many other iterations, each as unique as the situation. Tune into your space and environment to see if there are ways you can help slow the rate of flow into your receptors.

"Life is a balance between holding on and letting go."

Rumi

The Dance of Motherhood

To borrow Rumi's words and adapt a bit, *"Motherhood* is the dance of holding on and letting go." A fluid movement of push-pull, give-take, back-and-forth. Sometimes we know the steps. Sometimes we know the music. Sometimes it's an easy beautiful artistic display. Synchronized, light, and airy. Other times we stumble, can't hear the music at all (or it's too fast or too slow for our taste), and we're doing the truffle shuffle when everyone else is clearly waltzing.

As a parent, we consistently face matters of holding on (please stay little and snuggly forever) and letting go (please, I just want to get through this phase). This is so hard. A constant ebb and flow. A never-ending dance.

I present this idea as a dance because I think there is gentleness and beauty in the notion of a dance. The way the ocean and the shore are in an eternal back and forth with one another, so too are the parent and child. Thinking of it in this way allows me to see the beauty and the inherent challenge and angst that are all part of this reality.

Holding onto this idea reminds me that this journey is also non-linear and sometimes a bit messy. When I feel like I'm all out of whack and I don't know the steps, I am reminded that I'm not a failure—I'm just in the thick of it. I'm doing the dance. I'm engaged in the messy process of making art with my life. It's not *supposed* to look like anything else. This **is** it.

While this process is messy and hard, it can be a little bit better if you try to learn the steps. By all means, self-assess and seek improvement. Set goals. It always feels a little better to be on tempo and nailing your footwork! Get better. Read the books (obviously, I'm a fan) and the blogs, and take the advice. But also remember, even the most practiced and well-rehearsed dancer still misses a step every now and then.

Finally, recognize that it's never done. We need to know that the second we think we've got these steps down—nailed it—those tiny humans are going to grow and develop, and we're looking at new dance moves. Embracing the process makes me a heck of a lot less frustrated (and dare I say find the humor in it) when I've got the Macarena down (finally) and they're doing the floss (or whatever current dance trend is in style). Push-pull. Give-take. Ebb-flow. Dance.

"Shouting 'self-care' at people who actually need 'community care' is how we fail people."

Nakita Valerio

Self-Care

I have long been a critic of the standard self-care narrative. Too many mamas, myself included, feel that "taking time for self-care" is considered a "cure-all" and often something they feel that they're not able to fully or appropriately accomplish, which can often leave a mama feeling like it's one more thing she's not doing "right" and that's not good, plain and simple.

Let's get one thing out of the way, self-care is absolutely essential. I take no issue with caring for oneself through eating, taking vitamins and medications, general basic hygiene, and the like. These are means of caring for ourselves that are pretty basic essential life functions. And, yes, even at times some of us have struggled to do even those. These tasks are essential and necessary. My critique is distinct from this.

My criticism is with the narratives and social construction surrounding self-care, more specifically, when we speak about women's self-care and even more so mothers' self-care.

"Give yourself the same care and attention that you give to others, and watch yourself bloom." → translation: you are the reason you're suffering.

"You can't take care of someone else until you take care of yourself." → translation: you are not able to take care of your baby.

"Take time for yourself." → translation: there's enough time to do it all, and you just aren't managing it right.

Have you ever heard one of these messages and thought, *"That's it! I didn't even think of it. I just wasn't taking care of myself. Silly me. I'll get right on that!"* No! Hell no. What I mean is that no one is leaving self-care—that feels genuinely and readily accessible—on the table. Therefore, telling someone to practice self-care often feels like looking at someone with a gushing wound and telling them they "should get that looked at."

No one would disagree with the idea that taking more time to rest, indulge in hobbies, and socialize would be ideal. Personally, I'm a huge fan of taking a bath.[2] Hydrotherapy is my jam. It is self-care—absolutely! Do I love it when I get to lock myself in that bathroom and sink into that deep tub for 20 to 30 minutes once a week—heck yeah! When I get out of the bath, is my job (motherhood) any different— No. My child is still going to get sick in the middle of the night. We're not going to find that just-right pair of socks in the morning. We're going to forget that Thursdays the older one has band practice before school. Am I able to better handle these normal complications because of my bath? Maybe. It depends on the day.

The bath is great, but it's not a cure. It's not going to stop the hard and challenging realities of parenthood.

---

[2] Bath is being used as an example of a common self-care suggestion. There are many. Fill in your personal favorite(s).

When we talk about self-care as a solution to this big picture reality and then a mama doesn't feel better after she finally indulged in that bath, it can feel like a heavy dose of defeat. That's not good.

Stop telling mothers to take care of themselves and start taking care of them. If we see a mama who is struggling and overwhelmed and we don't ask ourselves how she got there and instead tell her she needs to do something else, we're failing her.

Don't tell mamas their tank is empty without acknowledging how it got empty or how to refill it. Doing so is dismissive and traumatizing. They know it's empty. They experience the emotional and physical consequences of its emptiness.

It's not like there are pockets of time available to do more for yourself and you're just opting not to do them. No. No mother feels this way. Mothers feel MAXED OUT. They are juggling all of the things. Mothers are both carefully and chaotically orchestrating hectic schedules (from baths to field trips to band practice) and more moving parts than they thought possible to not only hold their families together but to also propel them forward *every day!*

We often call this the "invisible work" of motherhood. It's all the things we're juggling and carrying around that often go unseen and unacknowledged, and we're often doing it without a village. I'll talk more about the impacts of community in Chapter 22, but it applies here as well. **Raising tiny humans without a village is super hard, and telling mamas that it will be somehow less hard if they'd *just* take care of themselves is highly problematic.** These narratives MISS THE POINT. They ultimately imply mothers are somehow responsible for their own state of exhaustion and overwhelm. Such statements fail to recognize that raising tiny humans is just really hard and that feeling this way isn't a personal shortcoming. **Our**

narratives can also imply that self-care will solve a broader problem: motherhood is simply exhausting.

So, where do we go from here? We've established that we need self-care, mothering without a community is extra hard, and our narratives around this subject can be problematic. It's a bit of a pickle, isn't it?

The ability to parse out these pieces can help us navigate these waters with a little more insight and awareness.

While I'd love nothing more than for everyone to stop with this current narrative, I know that's not realistic. Sadly, mamas, I think we're the ones who have to lead here. We need to be that catalyst for change. I know—one more thing, right? I think it's a mix. We need to change the narrative, but we also need to take ownership of our needs, ask for them to be met (by our community), and accept what is available or offered. Ideally, we need to do this **before** the seas are raging—when we are melting down and burning out.

Our needs and ways to meet them vary for each unique situation. So, go easy on yourself and be realistic as you reflect on all this self-care business.

Here are some thoughts about exploring this issue from both a personal and a community level.

1. **Needing a break is normal: You don't have to be everything to everyone all the time, mamas.** Know when you need to walk away and catch your breath, then make a plan to make that happen. In need of a break? Absolutely totally 100 percent normal. A gentle reminder that the baby will be okay if you do something for yourself. It's okay to leave your baby with a loving caregiver to go to dinner with friends, catch a movie with your spouse, or even head to the gym for some exercise. If that's what you need to feel good, do it.

2. **Identify and claim your needs.** What are you feeling? Get clear about that. Claim those feelings (get familiar with them). Consider what you want to do about your feelings. How might you be able to meet these needs? (Hint: there are often various ways to meet them.) A trip to the grocery store for 30 minutes can feel like a refreshing thrill when you've been dealing with a sick baby all day, am I right? If you have a partner who is coming home at the end of the day, be proactive. Let them know you need that escape/self-care session.

3. **Take inventory and communicate.** Who are your people (your village and community) and how can they help you? Then, tell your people (partner, friends, the grandparents, etc.) what you need and ask for help (as you define it).

   • Yes, you are worthy of this support, but it also may take more than one conversation for your people to "get it."

   • Yes, your co-parent and spouse works hard all day, but it's different work than you're doing [mostly] at home with a baby (or being the default parent, even after you return to work outside the home).

   • Yes, you have to actually communicate. We have to figure out our needs and then communicate them. Our partners aren't mind readers. I know, I know. Believe me, I wish they were. *True love's kiss and all that happily ever after stuff would be so much more bliss if they were mind readers!*

4. **Make a plan.** Be strategic about spacing out your helpers. Perhaps your spouse can take parental

leave for the first days or weeks. If this is an option, do it! Following their return to work, have another person (maybe grandparents) lined up to assist. After their departure, the other set of grandparents. Ideally, you could fill up that first month or so with this type of staggered help. Fill in with community members as needed.

5. **Accept the help, even imperfect help, when it's offered.** It's ironic how we may be able to get through all of the previous steps here and then, when our community does show up for us, we can be reluctant to accept it. Knowing what you need (help, support, love, rest, nurturing, etc.) is essential, but we've also got to be willing to let the people that are willing and able helpers in. That's on us. So, open the door.

IMPERFECT HELP

Imperfect help: friends or family who show up to love on you and your family in all their messy human ways. These helpers might come with some suggestions and advice that make you want to roll your eyes all the way back into your head. Accept it anyway. Annoyance, the need to roll your eyes, and even frustration are all feelings that shouldn't cause you to turn down loving and willing helpers. Significant and long-term emotional distress and, most certainly, any type of traumatic experience are well-founded reasons for saying, "no thanks." In short, accept the help. Let people help you even if they do it a little differently than you'd prefer. Accept it.

6. **Hire help.** If you don't have family or an extended network of friends or community to help you, especially in those earliest days and weeks, consider a postpartum doula. Hiring help isn't always an easy option, but their help can be priceless. Many doulas even offer payment plans or a registry to help offset the cost.

The mama's story on the next page is just one example of how our needs and the self-care narrative intermingle to impact our experiences. And while her situation is unique to her, the response to help (guilt) is common. Our cultural narratives often encourage us to believe that the need for support is a sign that we are weak, that needing help is a burden, or that we display incompetence if we need it. It's natural to want to reject it, if we believe this to be true. **What I hope for you is that instead of rejecting the help, you'll reject that narrative.** More about this in Chapter 21: The Rugged Individual.

Self-care means accepting that we're not meant to do it alone. Reconciling our knowledge about our own needs and what community support can look like may be challenging. I encourage you to reflect on your own thoughts, feelings, and experiences with the self-care narrative and the need to accept help as part of self-care as you continue navigating your parenthood path.

ACCEPT THE GIFT

A woman came to see me during her third pregnancy to work on some strategies to help her potentially avoid the postpartum anxiety she'd experienced after her last birth. We talked about many things during our sessions, and one strategy she'd put in place was a string of family helpers that would come stay with her postpartum.

After having her baby she made an appointment and came to see me. She came in with her older two children (ages 2 and 4) and a brand new baby (about 2 weeks old) in tow. She told me that she was feeling very overwhelmed and tired.

I asked about her support team, "Didn't you say you had a lot of family lined up to help these first few weeks and your spouse took time off of work?" "Well, yes," she responded. "Were they helpful?" "No. I mean, yes. They'd offer to help, but I just felt so guilty about accepting it. So, in the end, I just ended up doing things myself. I was hosting and entertaining them as guests."

We talked about her feelings of guilt and ways to view help as a gift. Just as we wouldn't turn down a gift someone gave us at our baby shower, we should not turn down help either.

9

*"True self-care is not salt baths and chocolate cake, it is making the
choice to build a life you don't need to regularly escape from."*

Brianna Wiest

Learn to Rest

I know "learning to rest" feels a bit counterintuitive with
a baby; however, learning to listen to your body and rest
when you need to can have huge benefits for your mental
health.

Our culture is all about hustling and bustling and busy-
ness. We measure success by productivity and output. Simply put, we don't value rest in our culture. In fact, we shame
people who rest. We seem to justify rest only after one has
earned it through hard work. "Work first, play later." Well,
that's fine and good except that the work of a parent is literally never-ending. When exactly does a busy parent "earn"
their rest? Yeah, exactly—never! We've got to understand
the powerful undercurrent of this message and assess how
much it might impact us. Try the mantra "It will get done
when it gets done" as a reminder that it's okay to slow down.

A couple notes on rest:

- **Rest doesn't always mean sleep.** There are
  many ways to get rest. Remember, your mind and
  body can do a lot with a slower pace and less on the
  to-do list.

- **Determine how to build regular rest into your life.** We can't operate well by going 100 miles an hour, resting for a hot minute, and then getting right back to racing pace again. Don't expect to avoid burnout by taking a pause for a singular moment.

- **Rest is not the same thing as lazy.** If you hear "lazy" in these words, you're listening to some damaging and dangerous messages from our culture, which reinforce productivity and output over health and well-being. You can prioritize rest and also be a contributing member of society who works hard and accomplishes great things.

Now is a good time to note that **MATERNITY LEAVE IS NOT A VACATION. (Yes, the capital letters are because I'm shouting!)** Maternity leave is about transition, healing, and **rest.** If you've given birth to that new baby your body needs to rest, heal, and recover. Pushing yourself during this time is not advantageous. Put on those comfy clothes, make yourself a little nest in a cozy chair, and hunker down to cuddle. I know, no one wants to stay in the house all day. I get it. Of course, go out. When you're feeling able and well-rested, go outside for a walk, wander around a local shopping center, or head to the grocery store. Just don't push yourself. Prioritize rest over productivity; you and your baby are worth it.

What about when you've got older children at home? I hear you. I see you. It's harder. It really is. Whether your older children are toddlers or school-aged, having tiny humans to care for is exhausting work and the idea of rest seems like a pipe dream. I get it. I'm not dismissing you. Challenge yourself to review your relationship with rest. I can't prescribe what this will look like in your life, but I do believe that a careful and curious assessment may turn up insights that can be valuable.

Figuring out how to rest isn't an easy task and won't happen overnight. Yet I strongly believe that a careful assessment and reflection on what rest means and how it looks is essential for all of us to undertake. Dr. Saundra Dalton-Smith writes extensively about the subject of rest. In her 2017 book Sacred Rest, she defines seven types of rest: physical, mental, social, creative, emotional, spiritual, and sensory. To truly rest, we have to be self-aware of how

I'm convinced that we've also become a culture that insists on vacationing as the only means to justify resting. This idea adds multiple layers of complexity. First, it means one must have the means, both the finances and employment status, that allow for vacationing. Second, is the very notion of a vacation itself. Most often this means a destination, somewhere we must go to be away from our life to justify rest. In general, our culture does little to promote the notion of appropriate and adequate rest in our regular lives. We must go somewhere to rest. It's easy to see how such ideas can be quite problematic and even promote burnout.

we're feeling depleted. Based on Dalton-Smith's seven types of rest, here are some examples of how to rest:

- Physical: chose a lower intensity workout; get up and move; wander in nature.

- Mental: meditate or try a grounding exercise (an example is provided in the extras).

- Sensory: turn off the lights/nosies (more about this in Chapter 6: Sensitivity).

- Social: say 'no' to some events; stay in (comfy social + Netflix + snuggly blanket); connect with reviving relationships.

- Emotional: surround yourself with people who make you feel like yourself; go to therapy.

- Creative: seek to be inspired; experience awe and wonder.

- Spiritual: work for a cause you care about.

Another rest practice is yoga nidra (also called yogic sleep). It's an ancient practice from India aimed at entering into the space of consciousness between sleep and waking. Think of this as a deep relaxation through guided meditation. Research has demonstrated that the practice can relieve stress and reduce symptoms of PTSD. Karen Brody founded the Daring to Rest Academy (see Resources) and has authored a book, *Daring to Rest*, along with podcasts, training, and workshops on the subject of yoga nidra and the power of rest. Her work stands in contrast to the notion that rest is "lazy, weak, and unproductive" and aims to "create a well-rested world" through yoga nidra practices.

A final note on rest: People often baulk at the idea of rest. It seems that rest has been associated with feelings of quitting or giving up. Challenge yourself if you feel this way. Refusing to rest in spite of your mind and body telling you to slow down and pause puts you (and your loved ones) at risk for suffering in the process. We can all agree that outcome isn't desirable. Learning to rest is wise. In doing so, you'll be more likely to accomplish your goals, perhaps because you were more engaged and present in the process.

Sleep

One of the most common things people hear about having a baby relates to how tired you'll be. It's true. Babies require a heck of a lot of attention and constant nourishment—as in, around the clock. Understatement of the year, I know!

Sleep loss is cumulative and is commonly referred to as sleep debt or deficit. Sleep loss after baby arrives is not like pulling an all-nighter here or there and then being able to catch up on the weekend. It's not like other times in our life when we've been tired.

Loss of sleep is associated with a host of conditions and/or disorders, and plays a huge role in how our human bodies function and survive. I feel like this whole babies requiring around the clock support might be a flaw in our evolutionary systems! A meta-analysis of perinatal studies indicated that sleep is a risk factor for perinatal mood and anxiety disorders (PMADs). Interestingly, a 2018 study from Zlatan Krizan, a professor at my home institution, Iowa State University, found that lack of sleep is associated with increased anger. A shocking finding, huh?!

Scholars do agree that the chronic and cumulative nature of postpartum sleep disruption is unique. Here are a few effects of cumulative lack of sleep:

- Cognitive impairment
- Irritability and mood changes
- Memory lapse
- Impaired immune system
- Increased heart rate

What good is knowing this when you can't do much about it? Knowledge is power. Understanding how much sleep impacts us, and especially the role of a sleep deficit on our well-being, informs our decision-making. It can help us be more proactive and protective of our sleep.

"Sleep when the baby sleeps." You've all heard it, and I'm guessing every single one of you has rolled your eyes at the phrase. If you're like me, you'll likely think, "Yeah, I'll also do the laundry and dishes when the baby does those, too." You've got to assess your own situation. Every baby is unique, and each household is going to handle this sleep issue in a unique way. Some babies are unicorns and fall into a sleeping pattern of four or more hours within a week or two. Yay for you, if you've got one of those (seriously, go play the lottery)! Most babies aren't this baby. Most babies take much of that fourth trimester to fall into a sleeping pattern that allows parents to start getting longer and more reasonable stretches of sleep.

Sometimes being proactive means ignoring the house and all other tasks and putting sleep first. I completely recognize how difficult and counterintuitive this is for some. If you find that you're starting to really suffer (some of the effects listed above), pull back and consider reprioritizing. One of the first things we can do to help ourselves when

we're feeling off is to check in on our sleep. Good communication with our partner and our support people is essential.
Ask for the help you need to cover the laundry and the dishes and whatever so you can sleep. It may be hard to have
to go there—to ask this ask, "let me sleep"—but it can be
instrumental in boosting your well-being.

Keep in mind that this is a phase. I know it seems like
a bunch of BS when you're up for the fifteenth night in
a row, but I promise you it won't be like this forever. This
perspective might help when you're feeling weighed down
and overwhelmed. I also know that asking for help for this
can be hard. I hear my clients say things like, "this isn't sus-
tainable" or "we can't do this forever" when it comes to
having a relative or postpartum doula or co-parent night
shift rotation in place. It's helpful to remember that these
plans are temporary and necessary. They can make a huge
difference in how you're feeling. And being able to feel like
a more functional and capable parent is the goal here! (see
Chapter 15 on "for right now").

Here are a few thoughts about getting the most out of
the sleep you are getting:

- **If you're able, don't turn on all the lights.**
  Dim lighting can help your baby fall back asleep
  quicker and easier, but also keeps your whole brain
  from waking up and acting like it's go time.

- **Tune into the circadian rhythm of light.**
  Our bodies are innately attuned to the rising and
  setting of the sun (and the seasons). Ever notice
  how you suddenly seem so tired by 7 p.m. in the fall
  when we've turned our clocks back (unless you live
  in Arizona)? That's your body saying, "Um...it's
  dark, we sleep now." Use this. When you need to be
  more proactive and protective of your sleep, tuning
  into this natural rhythm may help you. In our mod-

ern world, we use artificial light all the time. We've got the lights on in all rooms and often a screen or other device. Open the curtains, turn off the lights (and devices) and help your body cue into the natural rising and setting of the sun. This rhythm can help you fall asleep easier and get better sleep. This can also help our babies sleep (though, often not when their tummy says it's time to eat).

- **Turn off the blue light (our screens).** Studies have demonstrated not only how blue light can be harmful to our eyes over the long run, but also how it keeps our brains "on" (increases attention and reaction time) and significantly suppresses melatonin (our sleep hormone).

- **Lay low and take it easy.** Recognize that running all the errands and doing all the things might seem like a good or necessary boredom cure, but it can wear you out. Because your body is likely operating on fewer reserves, save some of those resources. I know being cooped up is hard, but you don't have to stay behind locked doors and closed curtains (usually). Just be aware of how hard you're going and consider how you can delegate and conserve more.

- **Rest doesn't always have to mean sleep.** Similar to the above, taking it easy and simply laying down (even if you don't truly sleep) can help your body. While we can all agree that a lovely eight hours would be restorative and ideal, give your body what you can when you can. Rest can also mean taking breaks. Add five more minutes to that shower. Seek out your opportunities to rest and snag 'em!

- **Try a melatonin supplement.** Of course, you should always talk to a doctor or, if breastfeeding, a lactation specialist before trying any medication or supplement. Melatonin is an over-the counter-supplement that can help support your body's naturally occurring sleep hormone.

Hormones

Hormones obviously play a role in our postpartum and transition to parenthood. But hormones are tricky because they are literally always in flux, not just during pregnancy, postpartum, or every 28 (or so) days. This state of flux means that our understanding of hormonal influences is somewhat inconclusive. We know they play a role, but the how and when can get complicated. Also, all humans have hormones, not just the ladies, though our cultural narratives often focus on them as merely being a women's issue. *We'll save that conversation for another day.*

Hormones are essential to our body's functioning. They tell our body organs what to do, when to do it, and for how long. They are our friends. In the simplest of scientific terms, hormones are chemicals. They are produced in our endocrine system, deposited into our

Fun Fact:
Non-pregnant and non-lactating partners also experience hormone changes related to having a baby? Yep. We even see neurological changes in our partners. Having a baby affects everyone involved!

bloodstream, and intended to carry messages about certain activities to other parts of our body. Hormones influence our growth and development, metabolism, sexual function, reproduction, and mood. Not so scary now, but perhaps still a little confusing.

Our bodies make 50 known hormones. These are further broken down into five or seven groups (depending on which literature you're reading). We'll focus on some key hormones related to pregnancy and lactation, as these are clearly the most relevant to our purpose here.

hCG

- Present as soon as egg meets sperm. Pregnancy tests measure this hormone to detect pregnancy.

- Tells our bodies to make more of other hormones, like estrogen and progesterone.

- Suppresses our immune system and funnels all the good stuff to the baby.

- Tells our bodies to stop normal "monthly" cycles in our uterus and to start making a home for the baby (the placenta).

- Many scientists believe this one might be responsible for morning sickness.

Estrogen

- Helps the uterus grow and promotes the development of the baby's organs.

- Can hit menopausal levels for the months after giving birth and may stay low while breastfeeding.

- Low levels can cause mood swings, irritability, hot flashes, and night sweats.

- Drops after birth and leads to an increase in the enzyme monoamine oxidase (MAO-A), which has been associated with reduction of neurotransmitters serotonin, dopamine, and norepinephrine, and may explain low or depressed mood.

Progesterone

- Increases to sky-high levels during pregnancy that can make us feel like we're free falling as they return to pre-pregnancy baselines.
- Low progesterone is related to anxiety, depression, mood swings, low libido, and insomnia.
- Boosts breast tissue growth, and helps soften ligaments in preparation for labor.

Testosterone

- Increases during pregnancy, but is generally lower during breastfeeding. Lower levels are associated with sexual desire and mental focus.

Relaxin

- Just like it sounds, relaxes the bones, ligaments, and muscles for labor.

Human placental lactogen (HPL)

- Prepares the breasts to breastfeed. This hormone, among others, is produced by the placenta and adjusts the body's metabolism to feed the baby.

Oxytocin

- Stimulates contractions during labor and can also give us a euphoric "drunk in love" rush after birth.
- *An illustration of this lovely love hormone is featured at the top of this chapter!*

Prolactin

- Loving those voluminous breasts? You can thank prolactin (along with progesterone). It's responsible for the increase in breast tissue size and for milk production.

- Calm hormone that allows us to focus and relax.

- Oxytocin and prolactin together can aid in relieving stress, increasing relaxation, and promoting positive feelings such as increased self-esteem and confidence.

> Fun Fact:
> Holding a [happy] baby for just 15 minutes can elevate oxytocin and prolactin— in fathers!

The ebb and flow of these hormones through our system affects us and can influence our mood and, get this, our sleep (among other things). Some hormones are linked with an increase in fear and anxiety and also memory loss (so, yes, mood swings and mommy brain are both real).

Here's a quick overview of what we might expect throughout pregnancy and postpartum.

1. The first trimester is likely to bring tears and forgetfulness ("baby/mommy brain"). Lots of mamas report a classic story of crying "for no reason" at a commercial. Normal. Totally normal and can be blamed on the surge in estrogen and progesterone.

2. The second trimester is usually associated with feeling the most blissed out. Ah! The glorious second trimester. Mood is generally high and even euphoric during this phase, not to mention your sex drive may increase!

3. During the third trimester you might feel more irritable. As your due date approaches, sleep gets more

challenging, which may be associated with some dips in your mood. The nesting urge also may kick because of increased levels of prolactin and progesterone.

4. The fourth trimester brings rapid swings in hormones (somewhat like the first trimester). Oxytocin and prolactin are huge players on the "up" side of things and are released when you're holding your baby skin to skin or breastfeeding. Estrogen levels can also take a dive postpartum, which may be one of the biggest culprits when it comes to low mood and depressed or anxious feelings.

This information has a lot less to do with what to do and more to do with comfort in better understanding. Hormone fluctuations are an easy target and a scapegoat to point a finger at when it comes to explaining the changes we experience during pregnancy, postpartum, or breastfeeding. Because our understanding of the complex interplay of these chemicals in our bodies is somewhat limited, it's hard to know just how to make yourself feel better when you're feeling "off." With that in mind, here are some general mood-boosting ideas relating to our "happy hormones" dopamine, serotonin, oxytocin, and endorphins.

Dopamine

- The reward hormone. This one makes us feel mentally alert. Eating protein can trigger the release of this hormone.

Serotonin

- The happiness hormone. This one is a mood regulator and influential when it comes to feelings of depression. We can boost serotonin through exposure to sunlight, eating carbs (yes, please), and exercising. So, eat a nice plate of carbonara and then go for a walk to get some sun! Win-win-win.

Oxytocin

- The love hormone. This hormone is responsible for increasing our feelings of love and trust. Oxytocin is released during intercourse, childbirth, and breastfeeding. While we know you might not be able (or desire) to do all of those every day, it's also released through physical touch, like a hug.

Endorphins

- The calm hormone. This one makes us feel relaxed and chilled out. It reduces anxiety and decreases our sensitivity to pain. Exercise can increase the release of endorphins.

These aren't all of our "happy hormones," but they are key players. This list isn't an exclusive resource of how to naturally trigger the release of these hormones. If you're curious about other ways to do this, by all means, head to Google and dig around. Trying these things (and others) are great entry-level interventions when you need to boost your mood.

In the fall of 2018, the brexanolone injection entered into phase three of clinical trials. This pharmacological intervention treats postpartum depression. It's a 60-hour in-patient infusion. What makes this medication unique is that it targets progesterone levels with a formulation of allopregnanolone. The medication targets the neurotransmitter gamma-aminobutyric acid (GABA) and aims to increase functionality of that receptor. It is believed that some pregnancy hormones can cause inflammation around this receptor and may influence the development of depression symptoms.

"*You are enough. You were enough before your struggles and problems. You are enough with your struggles and problems. Your hardships don't take away your worth. You are enough.*"

Elizabeth Kasujja

PART II

You Are Enough

Dear Mama,

You are enough. You are so enough you don't even know how enough you are. Any message that makes you question your worth is a message to re-evaluate. It's a lie. Yes. A lie. Anxiety and depression are liars. Perfection is a myth. And you are good enough.

Becoming a parent can really ignite or amplify imposter syndrome. Imposter syndrome, which tends to present most commonly in women, is a term attributed to two clinical psychologists, Dr. Pauline R. Clance and Suzanne A. Imes. In essence, imposter syndrome is an internal feeling that you are a fraud or undeserving of some role, rank, or accolade.

If you've never felt this way in other aspects of your life, specifically at work, awesome! However, it seems that even if you were a stranger to this feeling before, motherhood can bring it on. This has been referred to as "maternal imposter syndrome." Worry and concern about doing something wrong as a parent, inevitably "screwing up" your child, or simply being unworthy of the role as parent are incredibly common feelings. One key element about imposter syndrome (and self-doubt) is that it seems to present in areas of our lives where we really care about the outcome. Meaning, the more we care, the more intense imposter syndrome may present. And few of us would argue that motherhood is one of those areas we care about a heck of a lot.

I talk to lots of mamas about feeling that they are falling short or they are a failure 100 percent of the time—yes, really all the time. This is total crap. We're all being way too dang hard on ourselves. So many mamas experience these feelings because of their idea of what a "good mother" is supposed to look like, or what a "good mother" should say or do (usually that answer is all the things all the time, which is just bananas).

You've probably heard that you'd never talk to a friend the way you talk to yourself, and that's true. I take this a step further. Imagine for a second that you can step outside yourself. One version of yourself is calling the other you a failure. Maybe she's wagging her finger. Maybe she's raising her voice and adding in details about all the ways you're failing. Is the recipient of the lecture feeling good? I'm picturing her starting to cry. She may even be cowering a bit. Is this acceptable? Do you deserve this type of treatment? No. No. No. Not for one second! This treatment is NOT self love, tough love, or "just being honest." It's not helpful. It's not keeping you on a track or working toward a goal in the least.

Now let's imagine another version of you enters this room (yes, now there are three of you—stick with me). She's not having this. She's empathic, caring, and compassionate. What might she say to the lecturing version of you? I think she'd say, "Stop. She doesn't deserve this." Here's my plea, let that version in. Get out of your own way and open the door for the kind, compassionate you to come in.

Give yourself some grace and compassion. You are worthy and deserving of it one thousand times over. I don't have to know you to believe this is true down into the very depths of my soul. There is nothing in this book that I say with greater conviction and certainty than this: you are worthy of love, grace, and compassion, and you are enough.

With love,
Amanda

"You. Yes you. You are enough. Just as you are. Complete. Whole. Incredibly enough."

Frances Cannon

Supermom & the Perfection Myth

Dr. Carly Snyder, a specialist in reproductive psychiatry, stated that we can "revere motherhood, but that doesn't mean a mother has to be perfect." I agree with her. We need to call into question our ideas about motherhood, which means addressing the Supermom and perfection myths. Can we allow ourselves to love imperfect mothering? Most of all, can we disconnect this idea from the notion that anything less than perfect means our beloved children will somehow suffer irreparable harm?

So, where do our ideas about mothering and motherhood come from? Well, like everything in our world, they're a social construction. What building blocks did you use? How did you imagine motherhood would be? Donna Reed? Mary Poppins? Organic baby-food making, cloth-diapering, snuggle-fest? Laundry neatly folded and the clothes picked out for the next day before bed? Healthy meals served promptly at 6 p.m. with the whole family present? No yelling, certainly there would be no yelling! When it's

time for bed, the children offer a kiss on the cheek and hug
and scurry to their beds—you'll be in shortly to tuck them
in and say goodnight (no battles, ever)? I'm guessing you
can quickly make your own list here, but you get the idea.
A great way to eliminate some of these undercurrents is to
explore when and where you're using the words "supposed
to" or "should." I hear this often when mamas talk about
how something with childbirth or mothering was "supposed
to" go or how it "should" feel. I gently suggest challenging yourself to eliminate these words from your vocabulary.
They are emotional guilt-traps. They are not our friends.
When we start thinking/saying "supposed to" or "should"
we can actually activate a fear cycle (i.e., we are telling our
brain something is "wrong.") Instead, explore answers to
these questions:

- Why do you feel that way?
- What did you use (building blocks) to construct that
  concept for you?
- Perhaps more importantly, what does it mean for
  you? (i.e. why does it matter to you?)

**It's okay that you daydreamed an ideal of
what motherhood would be like. There's no harm
in that. We all do it.** This conversation isn't about tossing
out that idea. Rather, it's about having more realistic expectations and ultimately about raising our awareness of how
these internalized ideas influence us.

What is much more important to our conversation is
asking, how is that idea matching up with your own personal reality, and more specifically, how are you *feeling* about
that matchup? If you're waking up each day and feeling
like you're hitting that mark pretty well and giving yourself
a high-five at the end of the day—rock on! If you feel that
you're failing, falling short, and just not good enough and

defeated at the end of the day, let's explore that more.

How we reconcile our ideal with our reality isn't something that's unique to motherhood. It applies to any experience. Was the Eiffel Tower as impressive as you expected? What about the neighbors? Are they the "can I borrow a cup of sugar" kind you hoped for or more the "I'm calling the cops because your dog barked too loudly this morning" kind? Were the floral arrangements for the wedding the correct shade of pink you ordered? I could go on, but I hope you're getting the point. We have to engage in this reconciliation exercise in all areas of our lives. **What's unique to motherhood, as opposed to many of these other areas, is that our feelings here—our hopes and dreams and ideas—are all tightly wound up with our identity and what it means to be a "good mother."** If we feel disappointed or kind of "meh" about the Eiffel Tower, we don't internalize that feeling and ascribe it to our relationships or our own identity. We don't give motherhood the same consideration.

These ideas and internalized feelings can sometimes grow and amass into a Supermom archetype. A Supermom is someone who can (and *should*) do it all for everyone all the time. Generally with a flawless ease and grace throughout the process—never flustered or shaken by the need to, once again, thwart a villain or save the world! Supermoms are perfection personified. Guess what? The Supermom narrative is a total disaster for mental health. Shifting focus toward being a good enough or more authentic mom can be extremely beneficial.

British pediatrician and psychoanalyst Donald Winnicott coined the phrase "good enough mother" in his 1953 book *Playing and Reality*. Winnicott's work suggests that our children are actually helped by our humanness—meaning, imperfection is actually quite perfect! He suggested that manageable failures and shortcomings are actually the stuff of development gold for our tiny humans. Go figure! Every time a need is met flawlessly, we actually deny our children's brains the ability to use and build-up problem-solving cognitive pathways.

When we allow for a more complex world—a real and imperfect one—and offer our compassion, love, and empathy in the midst of challenges, we're doing more to further our children's development than when we attempt to create perfect experiences. Frankly, I think that's pretty darn great. And it gives me full permission to address this Supermom business.

"Good enough moms" recognize that life is messy and busy and that we're not failures when we have bad days. "Good enough moms" aren't chasing rainbows about doing it all. They're focusing on doing well with what's right in front of them. **The Supermom vibe is inherently un-**

FLAUNT IT WHEN YOU WANT TO

I'm a single mom of two kiddos with 1.5 jobs and I'm trying to write this book on the side. I'm hustling and bustling. Some days, I feel like I'm really kicking ass at this whole hustle and bustle thing. I'm pulling it off. I like that high (most days). I like feeling like I'm managing and I've got my ducks in a row. Yep! There are days that I put on that cape and flaunt it with pride. Hell yes! I deserve it. I'm pretty super. However, I recognize that it's not where I want to sustain myself. I can do it. I can pull it off, but, simply put, I'll burnout. I can't be doing all the things all the time. It's simply not realistic (for me). You have to figure out what's the just-right balance is for you. When do you get a sense of pride and accomplishment sporting that cape versus feeling happy and satisfied existing in that good enough space?

attainable and overwhelming. If you're struggling in that place, consider a metaphorical cape-burning session. You might feel better.

Hear me out, not trying to be Supermom doesn't mean you give up, don't care, or have no goals—far from it. It means setting more realistic expectations for you and your family. Take time to reflect on your relationship with this archetype.

Does setting new expectations mean that we should diminish the importance and significance of our role as a mama? Heck no! This parenting gig is important. It does matter. Of course, it does. And anyone out there doing this parenting gig is SUPER in my book. What I am suggesting here is to invite an internal critique:

- What's the source(s) of my ideal image? (The building materials I used to construct this archetype of the good mother.)

- How do I feel about those sourced materials? (When I think about these sources, do I feel more or less like a capable, awesome, competent, rockstar mama?)

- Do I want to reconsider how I'm allowing these materials to influence me? (Should I challenge myself to release some of these sources?)

- Are there other, "better" sources I can use for my building materials?

- As I become more aware of the building materials I've used to create this ideal image, how do I feel about the standard I've been holding myself to?

- Can I re-construct this image to be a more accurate and truthful representation that makes me feel good?

I'm not telling you something new when I say perfection is a myth and that the Supermom notion needs to be challenged. I know you know this, but sometimes we all need a reminder and encouragement to dig a little deeper into how these stories influence our lives.

I want to say one more thing about this Supermom business. I think you are a freaking Supermom. I don't need to know you personally to know that. The Supermom archetype isn't a problem because moms need to check their ego at the door. It's a problem because we can get caught up in the notion of chasing an ideal image that's entirely unattainable, rather than recognizing the awesome moms we are every single day.

My research participants frequently reported feeling that their friend, sister, neighbor, or someone else was able to do it all and with ease. I'm here to tell you, that's a lie. I don't mean that the individuals are directly or specifically lying. In most cases, this impression—that someone has it all together—is an idea we create, not something someone actually says or claims. Anxiety is a dirty liar. Anxiety is the voice that whispers, "Look at her, she's doing (fill in the blank) so much better than you." All lies.

The truth is, we've all got our own stuff going on. No one is really doing it all with ease. Everyone has their own struggles. My hard stuff might not be your hard stuff. For me, it's cooking; for you it might be bedtime routine or keeping your schedule organized. The fact that bedtime at my house is fairly painless might give you the idea that I somehow have my shit together or that it's easy. Meh! Maybe bedtime is, but figuring out how to feed my children lovely homemade, healthy meals every day makes me want to yank my hair out. We've all got our own version of hard.

So tell that anxious whisper to shut the hell up! I know, easier said than done. What I'm really inviting here is a careful and thoughtful evaluation of the source and truth of these messages (those whispers). Are they based on a lie or grounded in reality? Give yourself some grace, Mama. And then give yourself even more.

EMBRACING IMPERFECTION:
LEARNING TO LOVE MY CURLY HAIR

This is for all my curly friends out there. I have curly hair. I love my curly hair. In fact, it's actually my favorite feature. This wasn't always the case. Here's the deal: the catch about curly hair is that you never get the same hair twice. Okay, maybe it's not that extreme, and I know some of you non-curlies have hair trouble too, but just give me a pass on this one. I can wash with the same products and apply the same products after and if the dang dew points are up or down or who knows what I'll get a totally different outcome. And, as is life, on days when I'm least expecting it, my curls will look unbelievably amazing (those are the days I have no plans and am usually lounging about my house in pajamas, cruel irony).

Here's the point, my curls are beautiful and lovely and also unpredictable and imperfect. I can plan and prepare, but in the end, those curls are gonna do what they want to do. Choosing to love them despite my inability to control them and plan for their behavior has been an unexpected life lesson. My life is like my hair: messy, unruly, unpredictable. The more I embraced this truth, the less I worried and felt dis-ease. Sure, there are still days that I get upset and frustrated about it all (I mean, c'mon... can we get some consistency), but more days than not I love living in the messy middle of it all.

13

You Have Superpowers

Y ou have intuition. Yes, truly, even you. Intuition is a superpower. However, as a culture we often reject this notion. As Gavin De Becker writes in his book *The Gift of Fear,*
"Americans worship logic, even when it's wrong, and deny
intuition, even when it's right." To complicate this matter
further, anxiety and trauma can make it challenging to tune
in, hone, and trust your intuition. Remind yourself that you
do have an intuition (even if you have anxiety) and that har-
nessing this power as a parent can be very beneficial.

I know that it's hard to believe you have intuition, but
you do. It's evolutionary. It's just gotten messed up and
clouded for so many of us. First, it's completely dismissed
by our culture. Even reading this you might be thinking,
"Okay this is a little too woo-woo for me." But hear me out:
science actually backs me up on this one. Your intuition is
more powerful than you know. Our military is even working
with scientists to develop better ways to hone and harness
our intuition to help soldiers in combat situations.

Second, and especially if you identify as someone who
has anxiety or trauma, we are often taught to reject, deny, or

suppress these "gut" feelings within ourselves even when we do recognize them. To address this, we've got to recognize that intuition is an actual thing and start tuning into it.

How to hone your superpower:

- **Pay Attention.** I know this one is hard when you have anxiety or trauma responses. This isn't a suggestion I take lightly or make easily; it's hard but necessary. We have to try to sort out the messages attached to these feelings. We have to be able to hear what these messages tell us beyond giving us a warning. The data tells us that the more we refuse to acknowledge and pay attention, the less this superpower can help us. Our desire to avoid and suppress anything we've labelled as "bad" (for whatever reason) can actually have a numbing effect on our natural intuition. The first part of getting past that is to start paying attention and feeling our feelings.

- **Distinguish.** Once we start to really hear the various messages that we're getting and identify them, we can start labelling and distinguishing them—which ones are anxiety lying to me (because anxiety is a liar) or my own trauma response versus my intuition. I might have a gut feeling about something, but it's absolutely essential I learn to distinguish that feeling from a trauma response. A trauma or anxiety response is, typically, going to remind me that anything that remotely feels negative is bad. *Stop. Stay away.* When you can recognize your response is rooted in trauma and not your current experience, the more powerful you are. This recognition and distinction gives you the power to choose, instead of just reacting.

- **Be still.** Raising our awareness, learning to be quiet with ourselves, and what is generally known as "mindfulness" in the psychology field, is a powerful healing tool. I talk about these concepts throughout this book (you might even say they're a key theme) because they are so persistent in the data.

- **Be Curious.** Being able to sit back, be quiet, and get curious about our stuff can be challenging and hard, but both science and ancient wisdom have consistently demonstrated significant benefits to doing so. Being curious might sound like "I wonder..." statements (e.g., "I wonder what that's about" or "I wonder what the message is"). Once we are able to get a little deeper and understand our feelings a bit more, we can curiously experiment (e.g., "I wonder if I try this...").

Another great tip to help you focus and stay present is to figure out some core mantras (personal sayings) that really resonate with you. Keep these simple:

- "I am good enough."
- A favorite from Glennon Doyle: "I can do hard things."
- "I'm figuring it out."

When you find yourself about to get swept away in a wave of anxiety or trying to slow down and listen to your intuition, consider repeating your mantra to yourself. If you get distracted, return to it. There's no magic number of minutes you have to meditate, no number of times to repeat a mantra to practice more mindfulness. It can seem awkward at first, but stick with it and it usually starts to feel more normal and peaceful the more comfortable you get with it. If you desire, you can build upon your skills and truly integrate a meditation practice into your life in a more formal capacity, but you can also start simply to start reaping some of the benefits right now. Just like with any physical exercise, it takes time to build your muscles and see results. You'll experience this with mental exercises as well. Keep at it, you improve and strengthen your abilities each time you practice (even "failed" attempts count)! Welcome the distractions, as they are actually part practicing mindfulness. You don't have to completely rid your mind of thoughts for mindfulness to be successful and beneficial—that's why it's called a practice.

NOTES ON MINDFULNESS AND MEDITATION

There are many different ways to practice mindfulness and meditation (I've provided more thoughts on this in the Extras section). The terms "mindfulness" and "meditation" are often used interchangeably, as they are similar and interrelated, but the practices are different. In the most general sense, mindfulness can generally be viewed as your awareness; whereas, meditation is about acceptance of the present moment without any attempt to judge, add to, or alter it.

Meditation can leave us feeling euphoric. One of the reasons may be our minds are quite prone to wandering (some studies have noted that on average our mind is wandering fifty percent of the time). A wandering mind is linked to decreased feelings of happiness. Meditation can, in essence, combat this wandering. A calm and focused mind can make us feel better, happier. This focus could also be considered being more present. And guess what? Being more present is a key indicator of happiness. Meditation invites and encourages this presence. We are being present-moment mindful during meditation. The more we live in the moment (the more mindful we are), the happier we are.

Increasing mindfulness in our daily lives can prove extremely beneficial. We can be more mindful without cultivating a regular and systematic meditation practice. In the simplest form, mindfulness means to be aware or to pay attention. In most uses, being mindful refers to our thoughts, feelings, and behaviors. Therefore, to be more mindful in our daily lives we might simply increase our efforts to listen to our inner dialogue, name our feelings, or take note of our behaviors.

Mindfulness or meditation practices need not be fancy—and certainly not perfect—to be beneficial. Keep it simple and accessible. Want to know where I do my best meditating? The shower. Yep. it's my quiet spot (with a locked door) where the rhythmic sound of the water can help me "zone out" a little better. Hard day? Need to clear my head? Feeling foggy? I jump in the shower. That might not be your jam, and that's okay. The point is this, don't make it inaccessible by making it too complex.

On the days you're not feeling all that super, remember you have superpowers. Your intuition is real. You can hone this power through raising your awareness and turning your attention to it (mindfulness). Daniel Siegel writes in *Aware: The Science and Practice of Presence,* "where attention goes neurons flow." Siegel is explaining that our awareness can influence our brain functioning. Over time, we can (in essence) rewire our brain.

"The opposite of recognizing that we're feeling something is denying our emotions. The opposite of being curious is disengaging. When we deny our stories and disengage from tough emotions, they don't go away; instead, they own us, they define us. Our job is not to deny the story, but to defy the ending."

Brené Brown

Feeling Complicated

Our feelings are complicated and complex. It seems like a simple enough statement and one few would argue with. **Our feelings are not mutually exclusive events.**

In non-math terms, this means that we can (and do) experience multiple things (in this case feelings) at the same time. We can be happy and scared at the same time. Yes, really. You can be thrilled that your baby is here after a long pregnancy, but sad that you are spending your time with your partner talking about the consistency of your baby's bowel movements!

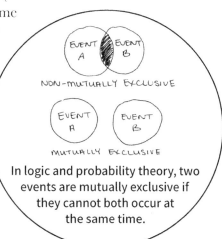

In logic and probability theory, two events are mutually exclusive if they cannot both occur at the same time.

I love that my pre-teen is gaining independence and can do so many things. It's exciting to watch. I have so much pride in bearing witness to these changes and challenges. That sweet baby smell has been replaced with a musky scent. And yet, some days I ache for that sweet child to curl up in my lap and allow my momma snuggles to wash away whatever ails him. Both are true. Both feelings are valid; they coexist and commingle. **One feeling doesn't negate the other.**

I hear from so many mamas about this struggle. We're so dismissive, as a culture, of these complex feelings. MadLibMom (@KaitlynNeath) tweeted this perfect summary of what I'm talking about here:

> **Me:** I'm tired.
>
> **Women everywhere:** Just enjoy the time with your kids. It doesn't last!
>
> **Me:** I said I'm tired, not that I hate my children, Janet. I'm allowed to feel things.

Mamas, you can be tired *and* still enjoy yourself. Or not (that's okay, too). This tweet shows society's lack of ability to acknowledge and allow space for the messiness of emotions. While such statements seem harmless, they really speak to a deeper, more detrimental issue. That issue is the belief that if I can have only one feeling at a time and if that feeling is negative, then my feelings of love for my child will cease. But that is not true at all!

Our challenge is to parse this out. If you've ever dismissed your own negative feeling (i.e., "This is so hard. I kind of hate this…") and tried to replace it with a positive one ("…but I love my child"), then you're familiar with what I mean. Getting curious and asking ourselves about the source of this desire to dismiss can be helpful.

- Are you feeling resistant to naming and claiming your feelings and experiences (specifically the negative ones)?

- If so, why? Where's that coming from?

- Is there fear that if you claim this stuff as pretty dang tough, hard, overwhelming, it means you don't love your child, aren't grateful for your child, aren't deserving of your child?

I hear mamas work through similar feelings all the time. It's important to take note that rarely are these feelings apparent on the surface. We're rarely aware that this is what we're doing. It takes some digging in and adjusting to fully recognize that we might be dismissing our feelings. So take the time to get curious. Dig in. Get messy.

Most of us want to always feel blissed-out joy about our new baby, especially in those early days. Most of us might have a pretty strong desire to avoid exploring complicated (or "negative") feelings about our journey as a parent. A happy family, right? That's what we all want and desire. **Our cultural narratives that fail to acknowledge complex feelings make it really hard for us to name and claim the reality that it's hard as hell *and* blissful.**

Having conflicting feelings is normal. Sometimes it's more one than the other. Some days, the bliss feeling is only about ten minutes and the hard-as-hell stuff consumes all the other moments. **It's hard *and* you love your child. Say that one again (and again). It's both.**

Why is this important to acknowledge? Our society might not be great about recognizing our non-mutually exclusive feelings, but we can get better about it within ourselves. In doing so, we give ourselves space and grace to feel all sorts of things all the time. I work with a lot of mamas who are sifting through guilt and shame because they don't always feel overwhelming love and joy at the tasks of motherhood. When we become aware and accepting of our feelings we are better able to release the oppressive and overwhelming feelings of guilt. When we tell ourselves, "It's both and that's okay," we're better able to address whatever challenges we face. Without the "name and claim" approach, we're left fighting invisible demons and feeling unprepared and overwhelmed at the battles before us.

Here's a strategy for engaging in the process of exploring your complicated non-mutually exclusive feelings:

1. **Feel it:** Be curious and let yourself feel your emotions.

2. **Name it:** Feelings aren't good or bad, right or wrong; they just are. Examine yourself and see if you can identify what it is you're really feeling.

3. **Claim it:** "I'm feeling..." Try hard to avoid attaching a "...but" to the end of this. In fact, instead of saying (for example), "I'm feeling sad, but I still love my baby." Try saying, "I'm feeling sad and that's okay." Give yourself permission to feel whatever it is that you're feeling (for as long as you need to feel it).

4. **Face it:** Make a plan. Are you okay with feeling that feeling? Do you need to talk with someone about it—a spouse, a friend? Do you need help to make it better, or do you just want someone to know you're feeling it? There are lots of ways to face your feelings, but we can't make a plan without the first three steps.

This exploratory process is such an important one for me because I hear so many mamas feel shame about their feelings or attach inaccurate details to what they're feeling.

This seems to come up the most when we talk about how dang hard and overwhelming this parenting gig can be. *If I claim this feeling, then I'm not a good mom (I'll be judged by myself and others).* In my experience, when we're able to dig in a little bit on what other details we're attaching to these stories, we're able to make better and more realistic plans for how to proceed. See also: Part III on community and asking for help (these seem to be quite inter-related).

FEEL IT. NAME IT. CLAIM IT. FACE IT.

I worked with a mama who reported a lot of anger (her word) at her husband for having to go on a work trip. She'll be left home with their 6-week-old and 2-year-old. After spending some time exploring her anger, she recognized she was really feeling fear. She was afraid that she was incapable of caring for the two children alone. The initial weeks with both children have been exhausting and overwhelming. She was surprised by this (didn't experience it with her first). She feared that these new challenges (and feelings) meant she couldn't do it as a mother of two. Her husband's work trip caused those feelings—I'm not good enough—to surge, and her response was anger. By being able to name and claim these deeper feelings (fear) and be curious about them (ask: Is this really true about me or is this just a "for right now" feeling?), she was better able to make a plan to face them.

I know that we don't like to feel yucky things. Avoiding pain is human nature. The problem arises when we do more to avoid (or not feel) our hard, yucky, and painful stuff than we do to seek out pleasure and good feelings. Here's a hard truth: healing (or self-growth) means you have to feel your feelings. **Feeling your feelings is one of the most powerful and healthiest things we can do for our overall and long-term health and well-being.** And it's hard. Necessary, but hard.

"Life is so messy that the temptation to straighten it up is very strong. And the results always illusory."

Anna Quindlen

Life is Messy, Get Dirty

When things don't feel perfect or different than what we think they should be, we might be tempted to isolate ourselves. That can end up hurting us. Willingness to get real with the messy reality is hard, but it can be your biggest ally. So give yourself permission to change and grow. We're always evaluating and re-evaluating our situation, circumstances, and choices. It's a reminder that doing something one moment or one day is not ***the*** decision, rather it's a choice you made ***for right now.*** It's an option taken for the here and now, not forever.

- "I'm taking a day off work for my mental health" is not the same as quitting one's job. It's *for right now.*

- I'm saying 'no' to that opportunity *for right now.* I might say 'yes' the next time it's presented to me (in the same or alternative form).

- We're not trying to have another baby *for right now.* We might feel differently next month or next year.

- We're not having a big family holiday at our house

for right now. We know we might feel differently next year, and that's okay.

"For right now" is about taking the space to consider your feelings and resources (mental, physical, financial, and so on) and making decisions that are best for you for the time being. Take time. Make a decision. **Don't guilt yourself; after all, it's just for right now.** Most of all, don't allow someone else's interpretation of your ability and resources to impact how you feel.

Sometimes the best decision is to decide to not decide. I know, counterintuitive! Sometimes, we get really caught up in the idea that a decision about something must absolutely be made right now. Take that idea off your plate and decide that you don't have to decide right now and that's okay, too.

We make hard decisions every day. Some are more obvious and weigh on us more than others, but they are constantly present nevertheless. We're no stranger to challenges and hard things in our lives.

Make the decision. If you want to change your decision, you can. You can do that. You can change your mind. Anytime.

Hard things are okay. We're not meant to live a life free from challenges like anxiety, sadness, guilt, or shame. These are realities in human lived experiences. And, for the most part, they are entirely universal. Embracing this truth and grounding ourselves in this reality can help you combat perfectionist tendencies. **When you live your life by giving and giving and giving and going and going and going toward some unachievable goal—perfection—you can hurt yourself, in both a literal and figurative sense.**

When we embrace the messy-imperfectness of life we free ourselves from the burden of shame and guilt that comes with believing we've failed when things are a little rough around the edges. This freedom allows us to be more present in the reality of our day-to-day moments without counting them as shortcomings.

Perfection isn't necessarily the problem. The problem is often that we grade ourselves on a pass/fail system. If passing means perfection, that means everything else is a failure. The issue lies with the grading system. You can still aim for perfection (if that's your thing), but consider that other outcomes deserving a passing grade, too.

This isn't the same thing as "giving up" and not having a goal. I know all you perfectionists are reading this chapter saying, "Well, what the heck? Just not care about anything, huh?!" Listen, I'm a recovering perfectionist. I get it.

What I'm making a case for is not the lack of drive and direction, just a realignment. Goals are good and necessary. They help us on a personal level, in our social lives, and in our careers. My critique is beyond having goals and instead is specific to the actual goal itself.

- Is it attainable and realistic?
- At what cost?
- How do you celebrate your successes along the way (not only at the end)?
- Are your goals shaped around how things are "supposed to" be or "should" be based on fiction? (And, yes, those Blogger and Instagram accounts may very well count as good fiction).

16

"You'll never know who you are unless you shed who you pretend to be."

Vironika Tugaleva

Integrate

If you've ever taken a basic introduction to human development course or a psych 101 course, you've probably heard something about the concept of nature versus nurture. It's the debate—which really isn't a debate at all these days—about whether or not our genes (nature) or our experiences (nurture) influence how we develop and who we become.

The reason it's not much of a debate anymore is most of our research points to the same conclusion: it's both. It's not only both, but it's also the *interaction* between nature and nurture that seems to be what matters most. What this points to even more, for me, is that we're really the summation of all of this. We're not pre-programmed DNA that will go through life in a robotic, prescribed manner, nor are we just a blank slate and our experiences the scribe.

Combining who and what we are into an integrated concept of self promotes our overall well-being. No more can we rewrite our DNA than we can toss out or forget our experiences. Sometimes that's a very hard pill to swallow. We want to forget about or push aside the bad experiences.

We don't want to think that they have any place in our life or in writing our story of who we become.

But they do.

Our desire to deny and reject this truth can do us more harm than good. These are common and normal defense mechanisms. We all do this. Our brain "builds walls" around bad things to protect us from the distress the negative emotion might cause. Similarly, we have antibodies within us (immune system) that fight off disease. Same concept, just in the mind.

I like to think about these defense mechanisms as holding an inflated beach ball under the water. It's doable, but it takes a lot of energy and effort (physical and mental alike) to keep that ball submerged. It doesn't want to stay under the water. Eventually, that ball is going to escape your grip and fly above the surface. Water will splash. You might get smacked in the face with that ball. It might hit someone. It will be a disruption. What I aim to point out with this metaphor is that our defense mechanisms work, but just like holding that beach ball under the water, they require our energy and result in some unpredictable disruption.

Our brains love certainty. Everything labeled. Understood. In its nice little box, on the right shelf, in the appropriate room (also, all clearly labeled and indicated on a map, of course). According to the child development theorist Jean Piaget, our labeling and organization system is called "schema." I like to think of our schema like a box with a label on the side. If a child has a dog at home, you might find that they'll refer to any four-legged furry creature as a "dog." Essentially, their brain is assimilating those other creatures into the box they already know, "dog." When children are able to distinguish a cow from a dog this is called "accommodating." They are making new boxes. And so on and so on with increasing complexity as we grow.

We get a lot of the materials—building blocks—for our schema boxes from the social world (revisit Social Construction in the Background section if you need a refresher). Meaning, we don't just go about experiencing everything as entirely new all the time and figuring it out for ourselves. If you had been living under a rock your whole life and were to walk into a university classroom, you'd most likely figure out what you're *supposed* to be doing in that space (assuming you're in the role of a student). You would receive cues from the way the people around you are behaving (where they sit, what they get out of their bags, how they speak, etc.). In some cases, you've already got some idea about what you might do in the lecture hall from social experiences like books, movies, and other media. These ideas—what something is "supposed" to be—influence how we feel about the beach balls that have been thrown our way and how we label them. (This is "good" so it can stay; this is "bad" so it must go away).

The idea of working toward an integrated self means assessing all the beach balls you're holding under the surface, and seeking to combine everything into a more complete and harmonious state. With my example, this integration might look like:

- Recognizing that you are in fact holding a ball (or two or ten) under the water.

- Sensing and feeling it (in your body). Ask yourself, "Where do I feel it? What does it feel like?"

- Acknowledging it by bringing it gently to the surface: "Oh, hello there, grief."

- Releasing it. It's still in the water. It's not gone. You're just changing your relationship with it.

- The currents will certainly cause that ball called grief (or sadness or anger or anxiety or whatever feeling you're addressing) to drift toward you from time to time and bump into you. When this happens, you can again acknowledge it: "Oh, here we are again. Something for me to think about, huh? Something for me to feel? Okay then."

Our energy changes when we do this. We are no longer trying so hard *not* to feel the things. To deny them a place in our story. Instead we accept them as part of us. **We integrate them.**

Lori Gottlieb a psychotherapist, New York Times best-selling author, and writer of the "Dear Therapist" column for *The Atlantic* states that "stories are the way we make sense of our lives" and advocates that we can become our own editor. In doing so, we can change our narratives and ultimately help ourselves get unstuck. In their book *The Spirituality of Imperfection: Storytelling and the Search for Meaning*, Ernest Kurtz and Katherine Ketcham suggest that telling our stories is where the power lies and how we release ourselves from our own internal narratives. Through the experiences (usually repeated) of sharing our stories, we're able to grow and move beyond them. The story itself (good, bad, painful, or other) isn't inherently problematic, but rather, our attachment to our stories is what impacts us. This "attachment to our stories" is the manner in which we're dealing with those beach balls in our swimming pool.

There are many different colored beach balls of varying sizes in our personal swimming pools. Over time, some may deflate, pop, or even sink. Sometimes we welcome those goodbyes, and sometimes we don't. When we look around and see the kaleidoscope of who we are in a more holistic way we free ourselves for other mental (and physical) tasks.

THE CHEERLEADER AND THE EMO GIRL

I've been working with a mama who is a self-described "type A perfectionist." She's a high achiever and very successful. The big issue she wanted to address was her negative feelings about having an unexpected emergency cesarean birth. We talked a lot about how she's always been able to set a goal, work hard, never give up, and achieve the outcome she desired. In many ways, she felt like this birth had been her first real "failure" (using her words here). Those are some big feels.

She came to therapy hoping to find some magic. She was hopeful that we could find some just-right way to swap those negative feelings for sunshine-and-rainbows feelings. She is not alone in this desire. Instead, we've explored ways to acknowledge all the feelings she's having about her experiences and integrate them.

She shared with me that she had two parts in her: the cheerleader and the emo girl. The cheerleader is loud and perky and reinforced as good and positive. The emo girl is sullen and quiet and doesn't really have much of a say. The reality of my client's lived experiences exists somewhere in the interaction between these two parts. Both of those feelings and voices matter in telling this story. One isn't good and the other bad, they just are. They're just feelings. Real, raw, honest feelings. As she recognized this, she was able to allow both of these parts to have a voice. She started to integrate all that both had to offer, resulting in a more complete and authentic telling (and feeling) of her story.

17

"Love is our true destiny. We do not find the meaning of life by ourselves alone—we find it with another."
Thomas Merton

A Primer on Attachment

I recently spent a weekend away with some friends. We're all parents, and while most of our children are older than babies, we turned our conversations to parenting in those early years on several occasions. At one point, the phrase "attachment parenting" was uttered. One of my friends quickly responded, "Oh, I could never be *that* kind of parent. The second I read about bed-sharing and babywearing all the time I knew it wasn't for me." Knowing this woman fairly well and knowing some of her parenting philosophies I told her, "You probably *are* that type of parent."

Attachment is one of my soapbox topics. I've been fascinated with attachment theory and practical applications of it since before I became a parent. I've studied it conceptually in various capacities, both formally and informally. It would seem that for most people—who don't geek out on the subject matter like me—they've perhaps heard of attachment in the context that my friend had.

In 2001, Dr. William & Martha Sears published a book called *The Attachment Parenting Book,* and with that a "new" parenting approach was born. The book outlined ways for parents to help promote a healthy attachment in their child. The book started a movement, and as with anything to do with parenting, it didn't take long before the suggestions were interpreted as a rigid set of rules with some folks "passing" and some folks "failing" (like my friend assumed) at meeting those requirements to join the pejorative club. I find that to be unfortunate, and what I had hoped to communicate to my friend that day is the core of attachment parenting philosophies (practical application) are quite in line with the theory of attachment. As with any philosophy, it's not intended to be taken as a prescription.

What is attachment theory, what does it mean, and why is it important? It's my hope that the theoretical concepts can be separated out from the lines drawn in the sand around defining ourselves as a parent.

Attachment theory is credited to John Bowlby and Mary Salter Ainsworth.[3] The core of the theory addresses our internal feelings of safety, security, and trust. In essence, how we each, individually, answer these questions can help us understand our attachment. (These questions are mine, not the theorists.)

1. What kind of place is the world (e.g., welcoming, warm, loving, scary, mean)?

2. Do I matter in this world (e.g., am I valuable and worthy of love)?

3. What are other people in the world (e.g., people are kind, caring, cruel)?

---

[3] As attachment theory has continued to be tested and advanced over the years (beyond Bowlby and Ainsworth's original works), there are now considered to be four subsets of insecure attachment styles: avoidant, ambivalent, disorganized, and reactive. While there can certainly be some hair-splitting in the child development and psychology communities about how the dust settles into each style and what testing measures are best, this general and oversimplified understanding should suffice for this context.

The conclusions we draw about our self (worth) and others (the world) is a simplified way to understand how we can measure our own attachment style. According to the theory, everyone has an attachment style, and there are two primary styles of attachment: secure and insecure.

As you can probably gather, someone with a more secure attachment style is likely to answer those questions in a manner that affirms their safety, security, trust, and value in the world. Whereas, a person with a less secure attachment may answer those questions highlighting danger, fear, mistrust, and feelings of worthlessness.

As you reflect on these questions, you can understand how parents and caregivers play a key role in helping us write our narratives. These internal narratives (referred to as "internal working models," but maybe best understood as "internal dialogue") shape how we interact with the world. If I believe (i.e. I have an internalized concept) that I am worthy and lovable, then I carry this out in various ways from my relationships with friends and family to the jobs I accept or leave.

TUNED IN PARENTING

I'm going to take a leap and assume that you probably want your child to develop answers that sound more like the securely attached individual. Here's the awesome part: parents play a big role in shaping those answers. That's why it's so important for parents to understand attachment theory's core ideas. **From these broad ideas, we can develop our own unique parenting style to meet the needs of our own unique children.**

Rather than thinking about rules and definitions of our parenting type, we can center these concepts as questions to *guide* us. Revisit the previous questions (pg. 97) and think about how you'd like your child to answer them in the future. That's it. That's all you have to do to develop your own guide. With this guide in mind, any parenting question or dilemma you'll face (and, trust me, there will be plenty) can be addressed by asking yourself, "Does this communicate a feeling of safety, security, trust, and value?" or "How can I promote a feeling of trust in this situation?"

Parenting with attachment development in mind means being tuned in. If you read about the theory, you'll come across the term "attunement," which is where the tuned in phrase comes from. Tuned in parents might tune in to some of the following things (remember this isn't a rigid or exclusive list, nor is it a benchmark for a "good" parent):

- **Learn your child's language.** Listen to their noises (coos and cries), body language (posturing for concern or comfort), and facial expressions (happy and content or tired) and what they are trying to tell you.

- **Respond** to your child with warmth and gentleness.

- **Validate** the feelings and experiences of your child.

- **Light them up!** This is one of my favorite ways to connect and bond with your baby. You know the way a little one can giggle and get lost in their laughter and joy. If you don't know what I'm talking about, do a quick YouTube search for "babies laughing" and I'm sure you'll get plenty of results. This is what "light them up" means. Sure, your tiniest babies aren't going to giggle, but that love/trust/joy response is still there. Try to turn that switch on at least once per day.

- **Gaze.** Even with the itty bitty infant we can connect via a good gazing session. Yes, literally just stare and gaze into their eyes with warmth and love. Smile. That's it. Start with a 10-minute session and go as long as you can. A simple thing like this goes a long way to building that tuned-in language. It's also great for their neurological development!

Back to my friend. Why do you think I said she probably was an "attachment parent"? Because I knew her to be a kind, caring, comforting, and responsive parent. I know that she concerns herself with communicating love and value to her children in so many diverse ways. I know that's she *tuned in* to each of her children and their unique needs. I know that her behaviors—even if she didn't bedshare, babywear, or breastfeed—are intentionally designed and carried out to promote a trust-based relationship with her children. That's what matters, not what we call it.

BE GENTLE WITH YOURSELF

Understanding your own attachment and thinking about how you'll use this knowledge to parent your own child may be an emotionally challenging process depending on your experiences. Go easy on yourself as you explore the ways in which your personal experiences with being parented will mix and mingle with your current experiences of parenting.

NOTE

Attachment is NOT uniquely or exclusively about liking or feeling bonded. I often hear people say, "Oh they won't leave my side; they're so attached." This is something different. Your child's preference for one parent over the other is not necessarily a good indicator of attachment style alone. This is simply a preference and could be present for a myriad of reasons. A strong bond is not the same thing as trust. Although "bonding" is a commonly used word when talking about attachment and does play a role in the formation of an attachment (so we believe), it is not the same thing as attachment. We can also bond with people out of fear and survival. The intent here isn't to delve into these other ideas, but simply to take note that these aren't quite the same or necessarily good measures of or indicators for attachment style.

18

What Matters Most

If I could offer first-time parents one piece of advice it would be this: it is not that big of a deal. I know that might sound patronizing and that's not my intent at all. What I mean is that so much of parenthood has been hyped up all to hell. Seriously, I mean it.

The nursery has the perfect color palette to be not too stimulating but just stimulating enough to make sure they turn out to be academic scholars. The right toys in the playroom that won't kill them, will teach them, and aren't made of plastic. Breast or bottle or both? Television and iPad time or no screen? When to introduce solids and what will those foods be? Should they sleep in our room or our bed and, if yes, for how long? Do I let them cry, or do I pick them up? Do we do the music class or the gymnastics class—when and for how long? Probably swimming lessons, too. No sunscreen before six months...

Clearly, this list could go on and on, and I'm guessing you're nodding your head along with several of these and could add plenty more. Feeling trapped, paralyzed, and overwhelmed by these seemingly huge decisions is a hellish place to be.

Rarely is there a black and white, yes or no, right or wrong answer to these dilemmas, which is equal parts frustrating and comforting. On one hand, I get that it would be so much easier if there were a manual—*Prescription for Parenting Your Unique Child: The Handbook*—to ensure the most optimal of outcomes. Well, there's not, and I know that kind of sucks. I get it. I am also warning you: if you're going to have more than one of these tiny humans in your life, they each come with their own unique stuff!

However, we can't really screw up. Yes! Hear me when I say this. Pending neglectful and abusive acts, these decisions—the ones I list above and the like—aren't making or breaking things. This is crucial to understand. In doing so, we *release that pressure valve* and can, hopefully, also release the grip some of these feelings have on us. Sweet freedom.

You can do all the things. You can take all the family trips. Enroll them in all the educational camps. Painstakingly research which sunscreen is the safest. You can. Those aren't bad things. Of course not. What's problematic is the way our society has sold (yes, and I literally mean *sold*) us on the idea of what a good parent looks like and what they do. Essentially, these decisions have been paired with the Supermom good mother myth (see Chapter 12).

I don't want to minimize how intense these decisions can feel. Every parent wants the best for their child. They want to give their kids every opportunity to succeed in life. Absolutely. The pressure to do that is very real. In fact, it's this intense feeling of making a "wrong" decision and the need to make sure that you're doing it all (literally) for your child that's problematic.

What is the solution? Pull back, catch your breath and assess. Ask:

- Where are these messages and pressures coming from?

- What messages are telling me I **need** to do these things to ensure an optimal outcome for my child (or to affirm my "good" parent status)?

- Does this promote or foster a healthy, secure, loving relationship?

- Am I afraid that if I make the "wrong" decision my child won't be okay?

When we become parents (even before our child is born), we are thrust into uncharted waters. These waters have currents that influence our course. The strong, "do it all *right* or else" current can quickly pull us under. I hear from so many parents about how exhausted and overwhelmed they are by the notion of having to do it all. Raising our awareness of these currents and adjusting our sails, if and when we need to, can help us take back control.

Bottom line: this shit doesn't matter. Not really. Not that much. Not in a big-picture kind of way. What does matter? That your child trusts you. That they feel safe and secure in their relationship with you (see Chapter 17: A Primer on Attachment). That they know they are loved. Period. The end. Yes, really. All the other stuff we buy or don't buy or do or don't do doesn't matter nearly as much as that one thing: our relationship with our kids. **That relationship is the foundation upon which all else is built.**

19

When Love Doesn't Feel Like Enough

There is an unspoken belief in our culture that if we just love enough things won't be hard. "Love is all you need," right? Thanks a lot Beatles! We say this about our relationships with our spouse and with our children. Is love a bad thing? Heck no! I mean, bring it on (see previous chapter). More love, always. What's problematic here is when this notion gets mixed up in the messy muddiness of real life.

"This feels so hard. I don't feel glamorous. I must be doing something wrong."

If you can relate to feelings like those, you're not alone. As I've mentioned throughout this book, these messages are socially constructed, and we pick up little bits and pieces of building material from all over the place (including our own childhood, social media, and pop culture, to name a few). What we need to do when we're challenged by these thoughts is to separate our love from the hard stuff.

You can love your child and not love the job. It's

a demanding job with shitty hours, no room for advancement, and very little recognition. Loving my child doesn't mean I'm thrilled to stay up all night with him. *I love you, but no I don't want to wipe your booty. I love you, but I don't want to do one more load of laundry. I love you, but I don't want to deal with your hunger strike. I love you, but taking you to the store with me feels like a nightmare.*

Love doesn't make the hard things not hard. They're still hard. That's their essence. Hard stuff sucks! Accepting this reality does not for one second diminish your love for your child. Give yourself the permission, the grace, and the space to say it's hard without any shame or guilt about your love for your child.

Here's what's important here: **Feeling like it's hard doesn't mean that something is wrong with you or affect how much you love your child and family. You can love lots and still experience the hard stuff.** In fact, I'm going to give you a money-back guarantee that you will experience both love and hardship throughout your life to many diverse and varying degrees. Does this mean you shouldn't seek help or support just because it's normal and expected to experience both? Nope. You can love lots, do hard things, and get help (see Chapter 26)—these are not mutually exclusive.

You Have the Power

Spoiler alert: After an odd and perilous adventure through Oz, Dorothy (and trusty sidekick, Toto) are about to depart in a hot air balloon for home when the balloon comes untied and lifts off without them. They're defeated and assume they're trapped in Oz indefinitely. Dorothy is devastated. Enter the ethereal Glinda the Good Witch. Dorothy begins to plead for Glinda to help. She quickly responds, "You don't need to be helped any longer. You've always had the power."

The number-one question I am often asked by mamas I'm working with is: "How?"

- How do I do this?
- How do I get through this?
- How can I start?
- How will I get better?

All of these questions are valid. All very normal and very hard questions when you're struggling. The specifics of how you're struggling isn't really relevant to addressing these questions, in my opinion. The answer to all of these questions lies within you. Just like Dorothy, you start with your own feet—you start where you're standing. You are on your own journey. Understanding where you are is an essential component to answering the above questions. There is no right or wrong in where you are—it's just where you are. Look around. Assess. Acknowledge. In doing so, you begin the journey.

I've said it before, but it bears saying it again: **Getting curious about what you're feeling is a powerful tool.** Having insight into your own stuff and being able to make thoughtful decisions about how you want to proceed is one of the most powerful things you can do for yourself. Don't get me wrong, I'm not saying this is an easy process. It's not something we do in a day or even a long weekend. Much like Dorothy, it's a journey. And, I would argue, one we're continually on in our ongoing process of becoming. There are people who help us along the way and foes (real or imagined) we must face, but ultimately the power lies within us. We decide. We walk that yellow brick road, or we don't.

LITTLE WINS

Working through your stuff and becoming aware of where it stems from and the standard responses you have (behaviors) allows you the opportunity to recognize there is room for alternative responses (choices). I recently had a regular session with a woman I've been working with for more than a year. She came to see me because she was pregnant for the third time and was having a lot of anxiety. She had a history of panic and was experiencing some of those symptoms again.

In fact, at times in her life, her anxiety and panic had caused her to isolate herself in her home and avoid work. We spent a lot of time in our sessions being curious about her anxiety: what were her triggers, what helped reduce her symptoms, and what was her anxiety trying to tell her.

During our recent session, she came into my office and told me about her "wins" over the past week. She proudly shared with me about an anxiety episode she'd experienced. She counted this as a win because she'd felt it and recognized it was "just anxiety," and was able to sit with it through that episode. She didn't feel debilitated or like she had to run away from it (as had been her pattern)—instead, she recognized that she had another choice. She could sit with it, wait it out, and see what happens. After all, it was just anxiety. It was uncomfortable, but she could manage that discomfort. Her recognition of her anxiety and choice to do something different didn't mean she was having a pleasurable experience. Rather, she realized she was in charge—not the anxiety. The anxiety subsided. She survived. She felt proud. She felt it was a win (it was). It might seem like a little change, but it was a monumental step toward recognizing that she holds power.

"*When we seek for connection, we restore the world to wholeness. Our seemingly separate lives become meaningful as we discover how truly necessary we are to each other.*"

Margaret J. Wheatley

PART III
Connection

Dear Mama,

The postpartum period is inherently isolating. And that's really hard. Whether you are a social butterfly or one who likes a small circle, doing something this monumental and life-changing alone can feel overwhelming.

No matter if it's your first baby or your fifth, postpartum can be a lonely road. We're often home alone with our babies trying to figure it all out. We haven't always done postpartum this way. In fact, we used to be supported by our community during this period. Our brains aren't really accustomed to isolation, especially during this transition.

Just a few short years ago—more like a century, but in the grand scheme that's not very long—by the time we became parents, we had already been an active part of many births and parenting situations. We were doing these things in community because we had to. By the time I was giving birth, I would have witnessed and likely helped with a number of births. I would have helped raise siblings, cousins, and neighbors. I would have been a part of a circle of women and other parents talking about birth and raising children.

But now we are disconnected from each other and from ourselves. This disconnection causes us pain.

While the forms of disconnection we may feel are personal and complex, on the whole, they are somewhat universal. These feelings of disconnection can be experienced in the way we have shifted to being dual-income households. Working parents who put in long hours can struggle to find ways to connect with friends and neighbors. We may feel this disconnection in the way our neighborhood schools are now conglomerates where parents might not even know all their children's teachers, let alone their peers and their peers' parents. We may feel this disconnection when we opt not to host friends and neighbors because we fear judgement over a lack of pristine conditions in our home. These feelings of disconnection are socially constructed and often culturally specific and can result in significant personal and collective feelings of brokenness for many.

I know this seems a bit extreme and perhaps even doom and gloom; however, when we dig in we can see the evidence of this disconnectedness or brokenness all around us in various ways (macro to micro). Through my research and my experiences working with families transitioning to parenthood, I have come to understand that connection heals us. Connection with each other—through our social networks—connection with nature, connection with ourselves, connection with our children, connection with our work, and even our connection with our environments (from our home to nature). It's all about connection.

How that's done and how that heals is as diverse as each individual. That's where things get complicated and nonlinear. Connection isn't as simple as going to hang out with a few friends this weekend to suddenly feel "all better!" Don't we wish it were that easy (and ya know what? Sometimes it is)!

In this section, we will explore some of the brokenness that results from disconnection and try to begin the healing process.

With love,
Amanda

"Humans are, by nature, pack animals. To be healthy and happy, we need to be embedded in and bond deeply with our human tribe... We can survive without this bonding, but we often feel a great emptiness, which we attempt to fill in a variety of unhealthy ways... to be mentally healthy, we must find ways of rebonding with our local human tribe in the context of a wider natural habitat that includes human, plant, and animal companions. To heal, we must break out of the artificial isolation that has been encouraged by the hyperindividualism of modern culture."

Linda Buzzell

The Rugged Individual

President Herbert Hoover is cited as having coined the phrase "rugged individualism" during a campaign speech in 1928. This term is used to highlight an ideal in which individuals are totally self-reliant and independent from outside support. He was referring to federal social service programs, and he spoke about this concept frequently during his presidency. In essence, he and those who used and expanded on the term were emphasizing the notion that strength, resilience, and, ultimately, success were the result of conquering hardships like the frontiersman conquered the west.

The idea of conquering the unknown as a means to claim "success" is very problematic. This concept, as it has been adopted and broadly applied, especially in an American context, has hurt us. As with any idea or social construct, we have internalized this notion and morphed it into a golden guiding rule or "The American Way."

I hear many new parents say they resist the help of family and friends because they want to do things themselves. Now, of course, there are benefits to figuring things out and finding your own groove. However, there are also tremendous benefits to surrounding yourself with loving and caring support persons. Keep in mind that our people are human, just like us, and their help will undoubtedly be imperfect, yet invaluable *(if we can open the door and accept it in this form)*. This works best when we all— the whole village— recognize that this help is all about supporting the mother and baby and not "taking care of my baby for me."

In many cultures, having a support system is the norm and the expectation. For weeks, various "village members" will nourish us back to full health (remember that giving birth and having a new baby is one heck of a physical and emotional drain), and help us as we adjust and transition. Chinese medicine has Zuo Yuezi ("sitting the month"), la cuarentena (a six-week "quarantine") is observed in many Latin American countries, and a 40-day "lying in" is a common custom in many Middle Eastern countries. See the resources section for a few suggestions to dig into these topics further.

Sadly, American parents often describe feeling that successful transition to parenthood means facing the uncer-

I like to think of this early help the same way we help our children learn to walk by holding their hands at first. We would never think of this type of supportive-loving-action as preventing or hindering their eventual ability to walk on their own. No more should we apply such ideas to help in the transition to parenthood phase as problematic or a hindrance. It's help. It won't be necessary or look just like this forever. Get out of your own way and grab that extended helping hand!

tain seas all alone. **Yet, in my research, can you guess what is the number one thing people say they need when asking about what would make their postpartum experiences better? More help.** We need each other. This is evident again and again in the data.

Several scholars have called out Hoover's notion of rugged individualism as inherently false. Among these is Malcolm Gladwell who said, "We have fallen in love with this notion of the self-made man, of the rags-to-riches story...and that idea and that ethos has permeated virtually every way in which we think about achievement, and I think that that idea is completely false; it's worse than false, it's dangerous!" Larry Eubanks wrote a piece titled "The Myth of the Rugged Individual" in which he argued that we are hurt by growing up with stories of individual accomplishments instead of stories of great collaboration.

There are a couple of things I want to examine here. First, yes, it's one thousand percent true that we need other people. As a species, we thrive in villages. We need connection and belonging. This is a protective evolutionary need. Period. Finding a village, in our modern era isn't easy, and I don't want to diminish the deep sense of loss and longing that can be associated with knowing the challenges of finding and connecting with your people.

Second, I also want to distinguish the need for community from the notion of being an extrovert, or feeling energized by being around people. Needing other people and also enjoying and appreciating—even craving—privacy can coexist. **Seeking connection does not imply loss of unique individuality, privacy, and even personal time and space.** Our need for other people also doesn't mean that sometimes we *do* need to do things on our own or that we're incapable of doing things on our own.

Finally, I believe it is essential to acknowledge that when we have experienced trauma, our ability to trust oth-

SHOW UP FOR PEOPLE

A mama, with a new baby, shared an experience with me about a friend who had older children (5 & 7) who had stopped by her house as part of a meal train. The friend could tell the new mama was struggling. So she asked if she could come over the next day just to visit, and she brought snacks, and held the baby while mama showered, and just listened. She wasn't a close friend, but the new mama described how grateful she was for that simple act of showing up.

ers is complicated and cloudy. Feeling that it is better or best to do it yourself because others can't be trusted is common when you've experienced trauma. What I'm suggesting in this section may be particularly challenging in such cases.

Here's this muddy middle we find ourselves in—this balance we have to seek and create for ourselves: the villages, for so many, are hard to come by. Multiple scholars have noted that we're living in an era where we're more "connected" (meaning digitally) than ever, yet we're reporting higher relationship dissatisfaction and loneliness. We have to first accept that we do indeed need other people and, perhaps, recognize that deep internal craving for these connections.

Next, we have to look for opportunities to foster and grow connections and build our communities, which is no easy feat when you're busy raising tiny humans. I get it. However, doing so, even in small *(that work for you)* ways, can be instrumentally life-saving at times.

Finding and building a community that fosters love and belonging is not something that will happen overnight (for most of us). It's something we must actively seek *and* create over time, and it comes with its fair share of challenges.

Diversify your means of seeking connection. What "failed" once might work the next time. What worked before might not work this time. Be open to the possibility of finding your people anywhere.

It's also important to honor your own timing. If you're feeling that absence of your people and your village, trying to meet new people might not be the best or most practical activity when you're two weeks postpartum. When you're feeling able, start. The timing is up to you. The flip side of this is also recognizing where and when you're in a place to help others build their village. Years from now, when your children are older, perhaps you'll be the one helping to cultivate community for others.

One basic thing we can all do is raise our awareness of how *the rugged individual archetype* may influence our decision-making.

- Are you resistant to help and support?

- If you are, what's the underlying message (or story) you're telling yourself?

- Are there remnants of this notion influencing you and do you want to adapt (i.e., not to buy into that myth)?

BECOMING A NEW PARENT AGAIN

There seems to be an interesting phenomenon in our culture that pops up in the data. The village (however large or small) comes out to rally around a family when a first baby is born, but less and less with subsequent babies. Our postpartum needs are no less simply because we've done this before. In fact, some might argue that our hands are even more full, which means we need even more help and support.

"It takes a village to raise a mother."
Ariell Alden-Danforth

Community

We are social beings. We have a deep need for connection with others. This need is more than emotional; it's an evolutionary need. Yes, I said *need*. We're not designed to live our lives in isolation. We are interdependent. We need each other for our survival. We belong to each other. This interdependency is as true for us as adults as it is for our children (refer to Chapter 17 on attachment for more discussion about what this need looks like in infancy).

As a society, we've really strayed from this interdependence over the years (say, the last few centuries), which has been to our great disadvantage. In fact, we intuitively *know* we need each other—as the common adage goes, "It takes a village"—and the difficulty in creating a village is detrimental to our overall well-being. That internal knowing and instinctual drive toward community is part of our collective challenge and struggle in our modern parenting. It's normal to simultaneously feel this drive and to also feel angst about our ability to address and meet this need.

Today, it's to our disadvantage that we're not doing things in a community. Somewhere along the way, the luxuries of the industrial revolution and discretionary incomes sent us into our homes, and the notion of privacy as a class quality prompted us to disconnect and close our doors. We started to think of other people's children and their lives as just that—theirs rather than ours. We stopped concerning ourselves with the needs of our neighbors because it was "none of our business." The result is that we have lost our communities. And further, on a personal level, we lost the feeling that comes from knowing our neighbors and knowing that they truly do care about us, our well-being, and our children.

Most of us don't really know any other way. In fact, hearing me say this might feel invasive. Why would I want someone in my life? You're right. Why would you? What does it mean to feel known and cared for by others? Does this affect our feeling of love and belonging and, in turn, our overall well-being? You bet it does. The loss of this hasn't come without consequences, like all things. The isolation of postpartum just highlights these consequences.

The known benefits of community have led some medical practices (OB/GYN and Midwifery Clinics) to move towards including group appointments as a regular part of prenatal care. These appointments typically include an education and discussion component where a small group meets prior to each member having their individual appointment with the provider. This allows time to ask questions, share information and experiences, and build relationships with others at a similar stage of pregnancy.

Loss of community is our collective trauma. Our brains—the product of millennia of evolution—are wired for community. Our brains (and our bodies) know we need people. We intuitively know we're not meant to do it alone. Our survival instinct desperately reaches out for community. When we come up empty in our searching, we experience fear (which can manifest in lots of ways). Cultivating connections with other people can be a challenging but essential task. In the next chapter we dive into some thoughts about how to foster these relationships.

"The brain is a social organ—it can only really be understood in relation with others."

Louis Cozolino

Finding Your People

I think I've made a pretty good case for how important social relationships are for our well-being. The strength of our social support systems comes up again and again and again in the data as a significant buffer (protective measure) and mediating factor (reduces the impact of hardship) when the storms are blowing. It comes up so much in the scientific literature that I find it practically laughable. **These relationships matter. They are important. We need them.**

All right, you get it, but you have social anxiety or feel insecure in these situations. These are an expected element of the human condition. Whether your circumstances and experiences are intense and severe enough to be clinically diagnosed or not, we know it's not uncommon to struggle with making friends (especially in adulthood).

I admit I don't have much anxiety around these types of social/friend-making situations; I did, however, grow up with a sibling and had a spouse who did. Of course, these are not my experiences, but I've lived in close and intimate relationships with people we do experience this kind of anxicty. I also have many friends and clients who experience struggles with these social situations. In short, for a person who does not experience these specific anxieties, I have a passionate interest in understanding and "finding solutions" to them.

Dr. Ellen Hendriksen, who lives with social anxiety, wrote in her 2018 book *How to Be Yourself* that the way to get past social anxiety is by going directly through it. What? It's like the children's book *Going on a Bear Hunt* (Michael Rosen, 1989): "Can't go over it. Can't go under it. Have to go through it." What Dr. Hendriksen offers in her text is that we can overcome uncomfortable situations by focusing outside ourselves. When we start to feel that anxiety build and we're uncomfortable, we tend to go inside of it. ("I'm uncomfortable; I want this feeling to stop; I need to leave.")

Instead, Hendriksen suggests that we focus outside ourselves—what's happening in the room, who is there, what food is out, what kind of lighting is there, what can I smell—anything that doesn't have to with that uncomfortable feeling. In other words, don't feed it by focusing on it. In summary, she states, "You get out of this by deliberately turning your attention inside out."

Steve Flowers, a marriage and family therapist and author, acknowledges in *The Mindful Path Through Shyness* that "it's painful to be anxious." As the title of his book might suggest, Flowers notes that while it's natural and normal to want to avoid and escape anxious thoughts caused by social situations, becoming mindful (aware) of these painful thoughts might be the path toward relief. More so, Flowers suggests that mindfulness can help us lead a more authentic life, or as he states, "can help you come home to being who and where you are."

"Mom friends" are the lifeboats when the seas are raging. It's super hard to make friends as an adult and even harder if you're feeling isolated or preoccupied since be-

LET YOUR WALLS DOWN

One day at preschool drop off, I was standing in the parking lot chatting with a friend when another walked up. Both of these friends were mamas of babies (as in, one year or younger at the time). The mama joining our conversation naturally asked, "How's it going?" My other friend responded in a bit of an exasperated way, "Kind of hard." I could tell my friend was a bit taken aback by the unfiltered and honest words she'd just let slip from her mouth. However, the other friend said, with what seemed like a huge sigh of relief, "Thank you so much for saying that. It's nice to just be honest and real." Let the walls come down, mamas! You might be surprised how many others appreciate having more authentic and real interactions with you.

coming a parent. I want to validate these challenges. However, I cannot encourage you enough to work through this and actively seek out "mom friends." Finding, creating, and curating a village of friends who are in a similar stage of life—raising tiny humans—who you can be real and authentic with is worth its weight in gold.

Give yourself the time, space, and grace to make this happen if you're not easily finding a village. Turn your attention to it. Are there places you can seek opportunities to get social and potentially make new friends? Go there—even when it's hard

"I've built more relationships with people by being open about my struggles than I ever could have pretending like I have it all together."

Jarrid Wilson

"I had really bad postpartum depression after I had my son, and it frightened me…But also, I didn't talk to anyone about it. I was very reluctant…My boyfriend said I should talk to other women who were pregnant, and I said, 'Fuck that, I ain't hanging around with a fuckin' bunch of mothers.' Then, without realizing it, I was gravitating toward pregnant women and other women with children, because I found they're a bit more patient. You'll be talking to someone, but you're not really listening, because you're so fuckin' tired. My friends who didn't have kids would get annoyed with me, whereas I knew I could just sit there and chat absolute mush with my friends who had children, and we wouldn't judge each other. One day I said to a friend, 'I fuckin' hate this,' and she just burst into tears and said, 'I fuckin' hate this, too.' And it was done. It lifted."

Adele, Vanity Fair, December 2016

and uncomfortable, try. Also, recognize that not everyone is going to be your cup of tea (nor will you be theirs). It's hard, but okay. You might also need to release some friendships that aren't serving you any longer. Let some go and make space for the people who are your people.

Here's a suggested strategy for cultivating new friendships:

1. **Set an intention:** You first have to decide that this is something you see as beneficial and want to do. Setting an intention opens you up to notice when opportunities to connect may be present.

2. **Identify opportunities:** Take note of invitations to socialize (whether formal or informal). Are there opportunities you may have been leaving on

the table because you weren't intentional or you weren't looking? When someone says, "We should hang out," identify that as an opportunity.

3. **Decide and do:** Once an opportunity is presented, take advantage of it. Act on it. Do something. If someone says, "Call me if you ever want to chat," do it.

4. **It's awkward, yes.** I once heard someone compare making friends as a parent to dating. It's awkward. You also may meet a lot of people ("go on dates") and find that not everyone is that "right match" for you. Keep at it. The hard work will be worth it when you find yourself surrounded by loving and supportive people who make you feel like you're loved and lovable being authentically you.

> "I was lingering by the diaper bags after Gymboree trying to work up the courage to ask another mom to exchange numbers."
>
> New mama trying to pick up a friend

My conclusion, from my years of work in this field in different capacities and my own experience as a mother, is that our lack of community and deep, intimate[4] connections with others is doing more harm to our emotional health and well-being than any other factor. Social support is at the heart of resilience. I want you to thrive, not merely survive the hard things. It's no surprise that when so many of us are feeling separated, isolated, and adrift that we're also finding ourselves struggling during

---

[4] I like this definition of intimacy: "People think that intimacy is about sex. But intimacy is about truth. When you realize you can tell someone your truth, when you can show yourself to them, when you can stand in front of them and their response is 'you're safe with me'—that's intimacy." —Taylor Jenkins Reid, *The Seven Husbands of Evelyn Hugo*

these transition times in life (when challenges are plentiful).

I'm sure you're thinking, okay, I get it, now what the heck do I do about it?

- **Attend the mommy groups.** Mommy groups are tricky. I'm not going to lie, they can be exclusive or cliquish (ew, I know), but not all of them are. Try several. Get recommendations from friends. Start your own. In general, I like to say we should give everything three tries. The first time is just awkward, the second time is like testing the waters, and the third should give you a deeper dive. If it doesn't feel right, walk away—that's okay too.

- **Meet the friends.** Get coffee. Play at the park. Be informal. Resist the urge to feel you have to perform. Fight back anxious feelings that anyone is judging you. I promise you, we're all just doing the best we can. If someone is judging you, that says more about them than you and, clearly, they're not your people. Move on and try again. Please, keep trying despite a setback (or two).

- **Go to the playgroup.** If you hear about a playgroup and you can attend, do it. One of the best ways to meet moms friends is to use your kiddos as a social buffer. It's a heck of a lot easier to talk about them than it is to talk about yourself.

- **Put yourself out there.** Reach out. I encourage you to reach out to others and foster those connections and intimate relationships you desire. Create your own reality. I also recognize how dang impossible reaching out may seem to many people for a variety of reasons. I get that. I hear you. I still have to put that one out there; it's valuable to set it as a goal.

- **Be intentional.** Sometimes simply raising your awareness of this need and setting an intention to find connections can be monumental in paving a way towards these relationships.

- **Get comfortable with messy hospitality.** I challenge you to not clean up and entertain a guest. I think this might be the number one surefire way to find your people: open your door even when it's messy. Let (imperfect, messy) people in.

- **Join the online forums.** Can't get out as easily as you would like? Try looking for your village online. I know many friends who have mom friends who "live in their phone." It's perhaps less than ideal, but a connection is a connection, and it's worth seeking out our people wherever we can find that. When trying the online forums and groups, try lots because, inevitably, some won't be the right fit.

- **Digital connection is better than no connection.** In addition to online forums, connecting with friends and family via texting, phone calls, or video chats is better than not connecting at all. Our brains can absorb the fact that we're loved and cared for, even if it's at a distance. Not having connection is far worse than accepting the imperfect forms of connection.

If you don't experience social anxiety, recognize this about yourself and look for opportunities to adopt [willing] introverts. Let's take care of each other, mamas. If these things aren't challenges for you, help out someone who finds it harder to connect and make friends.

NEW RULE

When someone you know and love has a new baby, reach out. Maybe make a visit. And when you do, ask the parents how they are doing. The baby won't remember your visit, but the parents will. Make them feel loved and held and cared for. They'll remember.

"Avoid comparison like the plague."
Jen Sincero

Social Comparison Sucks

We have *always* carefully crafted and curated our lives for public presentation. Social psychologists refer to this as impression management. This management process is the way we attempt to control information people have access to so we can influence the perceptions they have about us. This process happens both consciously and unconsciously. These behaviors preceded selfie culture, Instagram, and Snapchat. When school pictures involved wacky stray hairs or a tongue sticking out (as my second grade photo did), our parents scheduled retakes (usually). Selecting the family portrait to hang in the family living room was a thoughtful process. Even the images one chooses to frame and place on their office desk for display isn't just a random selection. Kings and queens of old had paintings commissioned and then redone if they were displeased.

One reason that human scientists believe we engage in impression management behaviors is because of our innate need to belong to a group. We are social beings. We've developed in community over millennia. From an evolutionary psychology perspective, we survive when we're in groups. Therefore, ensuring that we remain an accepted member of various social groups is actually a survival instinct. I know what you're thinking: "If someone doesn't like me, it's not like I'm going to be forced out of society and have to live alone in the woods." You're right. However, our ancient brains are still figuring that out. Our need to belong runs deep, and we're often not aware of how powerful this undercurrent is.

Like many people, I want a happy family life filled with giggles and adventures. Therefore, the images I create (through taking photos) and share (via social media outlets or printed in my photos albums…if I ever get around to making those) are more than likely going to reflect this desire. They're a projection of the story I want to tell. Is it fake? No. It is the whole story? No. Is it fair and appropriate to *also* tell about the "bad" days? Sure. Is it okay if I want to focus on the "good" days? Sure. For many, it can actually be quite helpful to focus on the happy or good moments when things feel heavy and overwhelming.

The desire to control our image (literal and figurative) and the access the public has to our image isn't new. Here's what *is* new: our access. In our modern world, in most cases, we're connected and able to access these images 24/7. We can't escape them. Whether it's an ad from Target in my feed or my friend's vacation photos, carefully crafted and curated images flood our worlds. That's the problem, not the images or the stories we're telling ourselves. Sure, we all probably see some "real" or "outtake" photos on our feeds, but, most likely, these are the exception and not the rule.

A parent, who may be at home with a newborn or up in the middle of the night for a feeding, starts scrolling. It's a very common and, ultimately, a benign activity most of us engage in. The trouble can arise when we start to compare ourselves to these images. When we start to say, "My life doesn't look or feel like that, I must not be okay." Boom!

Self-judgement, guilt, and shame join the party, putting us in a different mental space.

If you're able to look at these images and not think those things, that's great. For those of us who do find ourselves too often caught up in the dangerous spiral of self-loathing that can come from comparing ourselves to others, we need to be mindful. New parents who are often exhausted physically and emotionally are particularly vulnerable to fall into this spiral. A new parent may feel somewhat desperate to be reassured they're "doing it right," and when we're constantly bombarded by images that are well-crafted for presentation purposes, we may see ourselves as falling short. That's when things become a problem.

"A flower does not think of competing with the flower next to it. it just blooms."

Zen Shin

All right, so what do we do about this?

- **Take note of how these images affect you.** Perhaps you don't feel negatively impacted or you don't experience waves of self-doubt or negative self-talk. Perhaps you do, but you're able to recover fairly quickly. You don't get stuck on that negative loop. If you can look at these images and think, "Yay for them, that's great!" you're probably doing okay.

- **Limit exposure.** Feeling overwhelmed? It's okay to take a break. Step away for a little bit and see if you notice a difference in how you're feeling or your self-talk. You can set the rules for your break.

  ○ How long do you want to leave?

  ○ What social media accounts will you avoid?

You don't have to take a break from them all at the same time. Or maybe you want to quit "cold turkey" for a week or two. It's up to you!

○ Is it just a few types of accounts? Those fitness Instagram accounts might be a little tough to take when you're feeling already stuck at home with a newborn. For someone else, that account might feel motivating and encouraging. Take inventory yourself and set guidelines around your intake of these images that will best serve you and your unique needs.

- **Diversify your feeds.** You might not need to unfollow any accounts or limit your usage, but instead follow different accounts and increase the intention of your use. Following accounts that seem to narrowly focus on one type of parenting or life philosophy can lead to feeling overwhelmed and bombarded by equally narrow representation. Seek out other types of accounts. Diversity in both ideas and representation can help us remember that there are many variations of normal.

SOME SUGGESTIONS TO GET YOU STARTED

- 4th Trimester Bodies Project (@4thtribodies): Photo+Story-telling movement for Parents+Postpartum People

- Momming with truth (@mommingwithtruth): Encourage imPERFECT moms to ditch social norms & embrace their true selves

- Motherhood Rising (@motherhoodrising): motherhood is not for the faint of heart

- Motherly (@mother.ly): Born to send expert ideas and mom-to-mom inspiration to women exactly when they need it

- Take back postpartum (@takebackpostpartum): body positive, all bodies, variations of normal

- Emily McDowell (@emilymcdowell_): Cards & gifts for the relationships we really have

PINTEREST PERFECTION

A few months ago I was working with a postpartum client. She was a first-time mom who was about nine months postpartum. She made an appointment with me because she was concerned that she might be experiencing postpartum depression. As we talked, she kept mentioning how much she didn't look like other moms or feel like other moms. I asked what she meant by this and what other moms look and feel like. For the record, this mama looked like she fell off the pages of a magazine. Tan, tall, lean, defined cheekbones, a high brow, and eyelashes for days. In short, she would easily be considered by just about anyone to be very attractive. She clarified that she didn't feel like the images she was seeing. "I don't look like the happy mom in the Target ads" or "the moms pulling off Pinterest parties."

This mama is a great example of what I call "Pinterest perfectionism" and how the constant barrage of these carefully curated images can affect us. What she was feeling is what a lot of new moms feel. What she was experiencing was, for the most part, quite normal. Hard, but normal.

Your Changing Partnership

Here's a "no one told me" tidbit about your relationship after you become a parent: It's normal to feel resentment and frustration toward your partner after having a baby, especially when you believed this baby to be the most beautiful manifestation of your love in physical form (amiright?). A quick Google search for the phrase *"I didn't know I'd hate my husband after having a baby"* landed 120,000 results. Granted, we know most of those results aren't what I was looking for, but the first few pages of results are articles from Slate, HuffPost Parents, Today's Parent, and the blog Scary Mommy. Needless to say, it's pretty common and normal to feel this way. Hard, but normal. Jancee Dunn, author of the Slate article, wrote an entire book on the matter titled, *How Not to Hate Your Husband After Kids.*

Here's what we know:

- The research is pretty clear: the workload of managing a home (which includes child rearing) and the stress that comes with it, despite having awesome and loving and well-intended partners, falls mostly on a woman's shoulders. Yes, still, today in 2020.

"WAIT, THIS IS NORMAL?"

A couple came to see me because they were experiencing some relationship distress. They had two children under 5. During one of our sessions the husband mentioned that things just hadn't been the same between them since they'd had kids. He felt he and his wife hadn't been able to connect and communicate in the same way they had before children. The wife expressed that she didn't find their patterns to be an alarming or unusual change compared to her peers. I validated his concerns and agreed that what he was expressing was worthy of our attention and an area to work on, but not unexpected. Meaning, alone, it wasn't a cause to think that the relationship was doomed (as he had feared). He was shocked to hear this—from both me and his wife. He had no idea that the marital relationship would change in such ways. He mentioned that it was something he and his friends (also fathers) never talked about. Following this discussion, he reported feeling hopeful and relieved that his experiences weren't outside the range of normal. Hard, but normal.

- The "I'm doing it all" stress is often at the root of this resentment. This workload is often referred to as the "invisible work of motherhood," which I talk more about later in this chapter.

- Finally, when we know that it's normal, we are better equipped to deal with it in healthy and productive ways.

Another bit of honesty for you: parents aren't the happiest. Sorry folks. It's not what we want to hear when we think about being parents. Many of us would like to think of our babies as our love for our partner come to life so this not-so-happy news can feel shocking. That realization can be a hard pill to swallow, and it might even be confusing for some as maybe you feel so super happy to finally have that sweet baby. I'm with you. I delighted in my sweet babies. I felt full, happy, and satisfied. So, what the heck is going on here?

I teach a seminar on happiness for the honors program at my university and have also developed a study abroad program on the same topic. The study of happiness is a pet project of mine. I could go on and on about what I have learned about the science of happiness and even longer in the human sciences and mental health profession broadly, but here's the hard truth when it comes to happiness and parenting. Parents aren't all that happy.

Scientists gather data on happiness using a variety of measures. I truly don't want to turn this into a message about data collection and analysis methods, so, in short, we must keep in mind that these data look at trends across groups. This data doesn't say that parents are *not* happy, just that they are *less* happy than other groups at other times. This result has been replicated consistently in the data. Basically, life satisfaction takes a dip during the parenting years. It's kind of like a valley. Here's the good news, we don't stay in the valley forever. We get to the mountain tops again—right about the same time we become empty nesters. No joke!

Here's one way I interpret these results. One criteria often used to categorize happiness is freedom/autonomy/choice. As we were talking about this in my class one day, I asked for comments. One of my college students said, "I remember feeling so free when I got my first car. I didn't have to ask or really get permission. I could go where I wanted to go when I wanted to go." Later another student made the connection between lack of freedom, autonomy, and choice as a possible explanation for why parents of young children are less happy. Eureka! (See Chapter 5 on mourning).

Why am I sharing this with you? You already know this, right? It kind of blows that you can't go where you want to go when you want to go? I'm sharing this with you to validate that feeling. Feeling the lack of freedom, autonomy, and choice is a real thing. I'm sharing this so you know you're not alone in feeling like it's kind of a downer. Science has your back on this.

So what? I validated your feeling that sometimes you're grumpy, frustrated, and annoyed about this loss of freedom, who cares? The science of happiness also tells us that another key influence of personal happiness outcomes is relatedness. Feeling connected to other people. Or, in this case, misery loves company! Okay, I'm obviously being a bit facetious here, but it's ironically true. Simply knowing you're not alone in a feeling or experience can make you feel better and even boost your happiness.

This is where we can turn *in* to our partners. We are in this together. **It's hard for both of us.** Sure, in some pretty different ways, but also in many similar ways. We have an opportunity to connect around these challenges. In fact, it can be a real relationship booster to stand at the helm of your little boat and face these uncertain and tumultuous seas together, rather than further promoting our feelings of isolation.

Here are some thoughts about uniting around this hard stuff:

- **Admit that neither of you really knows what you're doing.** You're both figuring this out together. Sure, one of you may have more or less experience with babies or children, but you've never co-parented this baby before.

- **Set your bearings.** What are your shared family or parenting goals? Where are you steering this ship? Think in very broad terms when thinking about setting your course. Getting into the nitty-gritty details isn't necessary here.

- **Know your role.** Ships don't get where they

Your Changing Partnership   141

are going by putting everyone at the helm and no one at the sail. We all have different strengths and weaknesses. We don't have to share exactly half of a select set of specific roles to efficiently and successfully navigate the waters ahead. In fact, some might argue that knowing your roles and doing them effectively is better than trying to split up and share in each one. You'll have to decide what works for you.

- **What are we talking about?** Sometimes it's really helpful to identify the intention behind our communication. Are we looking to connect, commiserate, or problem solve? Figuring that out and often stating it upfront can be helpful in guiding conversations and meeting each other where we are.

- **Commiserate.** Yah know what can feel shockingly connecting? Finally, getting the baby to sleep after a rough night and looking over at your partner and being able to say, "Man that really sucked. Glad I'm in it with you." Acknowledging that it's hard and that you're in it together can go a long way. Maybe even toss a high-five at the parent who was finally able to get that tiny human to sleep.

Finding others in addition to our partner who are in a similar part of that valley can also prove beneficial. While connecting with others and commiserating about the challenges (including lack of freedom) may not get you out of the bottom of that valley any faster, it certainly might make it more bearable (a shallower valley). Find a pal (or two) and share your truth. Knowing that you're not alone (keeping in mind that our experiences vary) can be a very beneficial thing.

Note

It's important for me to acknowledge single parents and parents who don't have a supportive partner. I want you to know your journey matters and that you're seen. On a personal note, I can relate. I am a single parent now and struggled significantly with what support looked like when I was married to my children's other parent. It's safe to say that issues surrounding these unique and often challenging dynamics could be their own book. Nevertheless, I want to let you know I value you and your unique journey, too.

Dear Non-Default Parent,

I want to chat with you about the invisible work of motherhood and the business of being the default parent. Two distinct, yet overlapping, concepts that have a deep impact on our lives.

The invisible work of motherhood, or what is often also referred to as the "weight" of motherhood, is the mental load. The stuff that is seemingly (or literally) immeasurable, yet extremely emotionally heavy. The default parent is the parent the child(ren) will go to despite both being available and within the same proximity.

Once, my children (ages approximately six and two) were crawling and clambering all over me—talk about touched out—while their loving and available father sat on the same couch mere inches away. I was their default.

Being the default shouldn't be equated with the quality of the parent. This isn't about who is "better" or doing something "more right" than the other. It's truly just the person who the kids call and reach for. Try to avoid applying those other emotional components to it.

As well, just because there is a default parent— as there is in nearly every household (in single parent households, it's easier to identify)—this doesn't mean the children won't ever ask for the non-default parent or that the default parent won't flux and change with time and development.

Often, the invisible work—the mental load—is carried by the default parent. What this means, and the essence of what I want to get at here, is that this person can be easily overwhelmed. That person can get worn out. That person is doing things that can't [easily] be delegated. That person feels, perhaps rightfully so, that all they are doing is unseen, unable to weighed and measured, and therefore, unknown. It's hard to appreciate and celebrate the work that we don't see.

Here's what I know from working with families that struggle with these overlapping, invisible, and heavy roles: they don't necessarily want their partner (the non-default parent doing visible work) to necessarily DO more work around the house. This is rarely an issue of "doing more chores." In fact, I consistently hear mamas say they feel their partner does quite a bit around the house and to help with the child(ren). While certainly no one is ever going to turn down more to help, that's not what they are looking for.

What I hear is that they simply want to be seen, known, and appreciated for these invisible factors. They want their partner to know that the work they are doing isn't something that can be measured in baskets of laundry *carried or dishes washed. Their work doesn't ever have an end and is heavy, burdensome work. They want you to know that they need this work to be acknowledged because it's not easy. When you spend a lot of time caring for extremely dependent tiny humans, feeling seen, appreciated, and valued goes a long way!*

Here are some ideas for what this might look (or sound) like.

- *Genuinely tell her you appreciate her.*
- *Point out all the ways she's doing a great job.*
- *Mention that you love watching her love your children.*
- *Tell her that she's amazing and kicking ass (even if she doesn't feel like she is).*
- *Acknowledge just how much she does to keep the ship afloat.*
- *Just listen. Let her vent, but don't try to fix it or solve anything.*
- *Say you're grateful.*
- *Facilitate her getting a break—don't just tell her to ask for it, make it happen.*

With love,
Amanda

"Postpartum depression makes you suddenly feel like a stranger to yourself, but knowing the clinical facts are the first step toward wellness."

Judy Dippel, Breaking the Grip of Postpartum Depression

PART IV
When It's More Than Just Hard

As I mentioned in the introduction, this book isn't about perinatal mood and anxiety disorders (PMADs). However, PMADs are also common and very normal. As such, I believe it would be irresponsible and a disservice to my readers to not include some content on this subject. It's necessary to distinguish the contents of this section from the rest of the thoughts in this book—what I call "baseline hard stuff." This section begins with commentary on when you may want to seek help and concludes with some thoughts on what that help might look like.

Dear Mama,

Sometimes it's more than just hard. There are times when we have to acknowledge, often somewhat reluctantly, that it's more than just having a hard time transitioning. We're really not doing okay. We're too deep in our struggle, and we need more help. <u>You are NOT a failure. You are NOT alone. You ARE enough.</u>

A mental health struggle sucks. It's a bitch. Nothing I have stated in any of the previous sections or what I'll share with you here intends to make light of the challenges of parenthood—especially when there's an added layer of a mental health struggle or traumatic experience to process and heal. Nothing is ever simple. Some of what I have shared might really click with you and give you a new outlook and insight on what you're going through. It may also feel really superficial for the deep struggle you're in right now. If we had a one-size-fits-all solution, believe me, I'd make sure every parent had access to it.

This book primarily focuses on what I like to think of as "baseline hard" during this transition time. What I've previously highlighted are common experiences that resonate with most new parents to varying degrees. But sometimes we have hard stuff *on top of hard stuff (the waves are big and our boat capsizes). If this feels like what you're experiencing, you are absolutely not alone. A perinatal mood or anxiety disorder is the MOST COMMON complication of childbirth. I know it's hard and sometimes harder than hard. When we do feel like we've capsized (and, ya know what, even when we're just feeling really shaken by those big waves), it's time to stop and assess. Get your bearings. Regroup. Make a plan to gather yourself and right that boat again. This isn't a time to keep sailing as if nothing is amiss, yet so many people feel they must do this in spite of themselves.*

One of the best ways to prevent our hard stuff from getting harder is to familiarize ourselves with some of the signs and symptoms. In this next section, I provide a brief overview of some common behaviors to watch for and some information about ways you might consider addressing them. As stated before, this information is NOT a replacement for a diagnosis or medical advice. Diagnosing a perinatal mental health condition can be complicated and should be done with the help and guidance of a knowledgeable professional. I also discuss when to get help.

While I provide some formal thoughts on that matter in the following section, I also want to highlight my more succinct standing on that issue (which I elaborate on as well). You should seek out more help whenever the heck you feel like. WHENEVER. If you seek help and it didn't feel like the right help and you still feel like you need it, seek another source. You are worth it one thousand times over. Seek out the help you need to feel like the best version of you.

With love,
Amanda

When Should I Seek Help?

Whenever the heck you feel like it! Read that again. Mama (or anyone), if you feel like you might benefit from talking to someone, do it. If you feel like you might want to seek pharmacological (medication) support to feel better, do it. **The right time is when you feel like it.**

I won't speak to the specifics of medication interventions, nor will I dive deep into the psychological approaches in this book. However, I want you to know there are many different options on both fronts. If you do opt for either or both of these, know you might not hit that "feeling great again" bullseye right away. It may take a few attempts to find the right medication. It also may take seeing more than one therapist (maybe with varying approaches to psychotherapy) to find someone who's a good fit for you. Take your time and don't be afraid to say something if you feel like a treatment approach isn't right for you.

However, I do want to spend a moment talking about why I, personally, think someone should see a therapist.

"I don't know if I really need to see a therapist." I have heard this phrase often, even before I specialized in perinatal mental health. Sadly, depictions of perinatal mental health diagnoses in pop culture are often extreme or sensationalized examples, which can lead to misunderstandings about what these disorders look like and just how common they really are. These damaging examples can make it difficult to determine when seeing a therapist could potentially be beneficial. We can easily—and naturally—compare ourselves to *these* popular examples and think, "Well, I'm nothing like *that*" or "I'm not *that* bad" and decide that we must not need help.

Here's my stance: everyone can benefit from therapy. You're so shocked, right? Of course the therapist would say everyone can benefit! If there is any way that I could possibly convince you that this isn't just a sales pitch, it's that I too see a therapist on the regular. I'm not going through any major crisis or struggling with big adjustments *right now.* I have pretty good coping skills and a great support system *right now.* By many measures, you could argue that I don't *need* to see a therapist *right now.*

So why do I regularly see a therapist? It's beneficial! I see a therapist because it's someone to talk to about all my stuff. Silly stuff. Serious stuff. Confusing stuff. Decision stuff. Heavy stuff. Sad stuff. All the stuff!

A therapist is simply an outside source, another frame of reference, and a supportive therapeutic relationship. **Seeing a therapist means I have someone who lets me talk or cry or complain about any little thing I feel like with warmth and nurturance.** Sometimes I need help to see things another way or try a new approach, but sometimes I just need someone to listen to me. For me, I really need to process things out loud, and a therapist is an outstanding sounding board for this process.

I see clients often who just need to talk to somebody. That's it. It's that simple. They don't necessarily meet the criteria to be diagnosed with depression, anxiety, or any other condition. They just need to talk and process with someone. If you feel like you have pent up thoughts and feelings and you just don't want to "dump" all that on your friends or family (or don't feel you can), then seeing a therapist is a great idea. That's what we're here for—to listen to you. The therapeutic relationship is a safe container for everything swirling around in your head.

I have many clients who see me a few times. We establish rapport, work on some bits and pieces, and then we move to a "call me when you need me" schedule. When it comes to processing your childbirth experience, you might need to talk, but you might not need to be in therapy on a long-term, regular, ongoing basis. **After a baby is born it becomes all about the baby, of course. But sometimes the parent(s) need to talk about how they are feeling and not just how many times the baby had a bowel movement! That's what I'm here for.**

I tell all my clients, "You're in the driver's seat." It's up to the individual to determine what they need and want when it comes to our appointments. It's not uncommon to need only a few "check-in" sessions to let it all out! For others, even when things seem pretty steady or normal (or whatever word you'd like to use), they like the comfort of knowing a "get it all out" session is coming up once or twice a month.

In short, if you feel like you could benefit from a good vent session with a neutral party, you could benefit from seeing a therapist. Anybody could.

Perinatal Mood & Anxiety Disorders

The term perinatal mood and anxiety (PMAD) is used by the clinical and scientific community to describe the range of disorders that may present during the perinatal period. Previously, the term postpartum depression was primarily used to describe these perinatal disorders. Perinatal is a term used to refer to the period of time surrounding pregnancy and the year following birth. PMADs include major depression, anxiety, adjustment, bipolar, post-traumatic stress disorder (PTSD), and psychosis.

Approximately twenty percent of new mothers will experience PMADs. A 2018 NIH-led Federal task force on PMADs stated, "It has been repeatedly substantiated that Perinatal Mood and Anxiety Disorders are the most common complication surrounding childbirth, yet all too often it goes unrecognized and untreated." A woman is more likely to develop depression or anxiety during the first year after childbirth than at any other time in their life. And one in five postpartum maternal deaths is a suicide.

Additionally, around ten percent of fathers will experience a PMAD. A key risk factor for a father or partner to be diagnosed with a postpartum disorder is a mom who has one. Half of men who experience a PMAD had a partner with it. Meaning, protecting moms against the impacts of a PMAD would reduce the impact on partners. This information really speaks to our interconnectedness as partners and parents.

Parental mental health can also impact child development.

Needless to say, it's a big deal, and we want to do everything we can to prevent, identify, and treat these disorders.

PREVENTION

One of the best ways to prevent a PMAD is to be aware of the risk factors and be vigilant about monitoring. Some biological risk factors include hormone changes, genetics, a personal or family history of a mental health disorder, and previously having a PMAD. Some social and psychological risks include socioeconomic status, lack of support, unintended pregnancy, relationship stress, perfectionism, and social media (yes, really). Other factors include lack of sleep, nutrition, and overall health (of both mother and baby). It's important to also consider a few other factors. We know that race is correlated with higher rates of PMADs. Depression and anxiety are higher among women of color than white women. Black and Latinx women are also less likely to seek support, treatment, and follow-up after an initial psychiatric appointment. This indicates unmet needs for culturally respectful and appropriate services for these communities. Families who experience a neonatal intensive care unit (NICU) also have higher prevalence rates and more elevated symptomatology. In fact, NICU mothers have double the risk of developing a PMAD.

IDENTIFICATION

Perinatal mood and anxiety disorders can present at any time during the first two years after birth. This is somewhat debated in the literature; however, what's important here is risk can persist. In general, we know that the peak risk for a PMAD is the first four to six months after birth.

"Baby Blues"

Having the baby blues is very common and normal. Eighty percent of all women experience symptoms of the baby blues. These normal mood changes typically last for the first few weeks after birth and are generally associated with rapid fluctuations in hormones following birth (review Chapter 11: Hormones). Experiencing the baby blues typically does not impair a mother's ability to care for herself or her newborn (albeit challenging because it's still hard). Most women report sadness and crying, feeling overwhelmed, anxiousness and nervousness. Some women describe these symptoms as bad PMS and others reference feeling foggy during this time period. These symptoms typically dissipate after the first couple of weeks after birth. Just because the baby blues is not an official clinical diagnosis does not mean there are no benefits from various interventions and treatments.

Depression

Depression is the most widely known PMAD and also the most common. Some of the most common symptoms of perinatal depression include feeling overwhelmed, irritable, or angry. People who are experiencing depression often have sleep disturbances. In the case of depression (versus anxiety disorders), people are often "over sleeping" or struggling to get out of bed and go about their day. This is distinct from feeling tired or exhausted from lack of sleep. Another common feature of perinatal depression is apathy or lack of feelings toward the baby. Sometimes perinatal depression presents as "anxious depression." Like many other PMADs, this disorder may start during pregnancy but can occur anytime during the first year after giving birth (and sometimes beyond).

Anxiety

While perinatal depression is the most common and most well known of all the PMADs, anxiety is not far behind. Now that we're learning more about how this disorder presents during the perinatal period, I wouldn't be surprised if it surpasses depression for the top spot in the next decade.

Anxiety symptoms may include low appetite and insomnia. Again, there is a need to distinguish these beyond not sleeping because the baby is keeping you up and not eating because you're busy tending to the needs of the baby. This is about being tired and unable to sleep because anxious thoughts may keep you alert or having no desire to eat despite options being available.

Anxiety may leave someone feeling a sense of impending doom or with heightened fears and excessive worry. These often center around losing control, danger, or illnesses. Many people who experience anxiety, especially in the perinatal period, have a strong desire to stay home and/or a general fear of public places. Symptoms may cause someone to feel shaky or dizzy, or have shortness of breath. Keep in mind, that worry comes with the territory of parenthood—it's a brutal truth. And anxiety and stress are normal functions of our human brains. However, here we're talking about an inability for that normal system to "shut off." Worry and stress may consume your daily activities and prevent you from enjoying your life.

I want to talk for a moment about distinguishing worry from anxiety. **Here's a fact: if you have a child, you're going to worry.** Yep. You may be familiar with the words of Elizabeth Stone, author of *A Boy I Once Knew,* which summarizes this well, "Making the decision to have a child is momentous. It is to decide forever to have your heart go walking around outside your body." Worry or concern about your child's well-being is normal. While it's common to feel or say that these worries, at times, certainly make you anxious or stressed, it's generally distinguishable from anxiety in its persistence and severity.

Worry and concern for your child will be present, but easily managed or subtle. Worry is like a gentle rolling wave. Noticeable, but you can still sail those waters with relative ease. Anxiety is loud and disruptive. Anxiety feels like big waves knocking your little boat around often and for long periods of time (especially when it might not make sense that you'd be concerned or worried). Worry feels like part of that normal and natural dance of motherhood discussed in Chapter 7. There's a bit of a constant give and take. Go my child: grow, learn, and confidently leave the nest. Oh man, please be okay, be careful, do you have clean underwear! Anxiety persists beyond this. See Extras for some tips to try if you're struggling with anxiety.

Postpartum Rage

This one often falls into the category of "no one told me." Feeling frustrated and overwhelmed, to varying degrees, is fairly normal. However, for some parents, their frustrations may escalate and they feel rage. A phrase that is common for those who experience postpartum rage to express is, "I hated everything and everyone." Many who report rage often indicate that their feelings of rage were triggered by something that, in hindsight, was insignificant.

Generally, this rage feeling is associated with postpartum depression or anxiety (a subcategory), but it may present even when the criteria for these diagnoses is not met. A 2018 study from the University of British Columbia reported that those who experienced a perinatal mood or anxiety disorder were more likely to report feeling angry. They would often report this anger as "intense rage." One of the reasons our awareness about postpartum rage is important is feeling angry or rage may be a red flag that's missed when diagnosing a perinatal mood or anxiety disorder. Many who may be suffering from a PMAD don't think they have depression or anxiety because they feel mad and not sad. Therefore, they may not seek help or if they are being screened for PMADs they won't note these feelings because they believe them to be irrelevant.

Obsessive-Compulsive (OCD)

OCD is an anxiety disorder, and it's absolutely not the same thing as being neat, orderly, or particular. One of the key symptoms of OCD is a compulsive ritual (these are the repetitive behaviors many of us are familiar with). These rituals are specifically aimed at relieving anxiety. A person who is experiencing perinatal OCD may be extremely hyper-vigilant, fear being left alone, and have intrusive, repetitive thoughts (often scary in nature).

> To clarify: Scary thoughts are general worry or concern that something will happen to the baby or you (preventing you from caring for the baby). Having these occasional (and passing) scary thoughts are common and normal. Karen Klieman, author, PMADS expert, and founder of The Postpartum Stress Center published *Good Moms Have Scary Thoughts* in 2019, which is a lovely picture book (yes) aimed at normalizing these experiences. However, someone with OCD may become fixated on the horrifying nature of these scary thoughts. Someone with OCD doesn't have occasional or passing scary thoughts; the thoughts persist, are

overwhelming, and begin to significantly influence behaviors. Someone experiencing OCD fears that if they do not engage in a behavior (compulsive ritual) something bad will happen. Meaning, they must do the thing (e.g., wash the baby bottles three times) or else.

Posttraumatic Stress Disorder (PTSD)

Recognizing trauma in the perinatal period is a bit of a good news/bad news scenario. It's good because we can get people better help. It's bad because, well, it's trauma. Although understanding antecedents is important in any situation, it's particularly true with trauma disorders. In the case of trauma, it's much easier to say "X caused Y," whereas it's not always that clear with other situations.

However, like in any circumstances, people are complex beings and what may be traumatic for one person is not for another. That's okay. We each walk our own unique path with our own complex and messy feelings about what we're going through.

With that being said, here are some common experiences that may cause trauma responses: pregnancy loss, preterm or stillbirth, and infant loss. A frightening or life-threatening birth experience can also lead to trauma symptoms. Families who have neonatal intensive care (NICU) admission have double the risk for a PMAD, and trauma symptoms are very common (sidenote: this group deserves so much more love and attention than they are getting).

One of the most important things to note when it comes to trauma disorders is that perception is what matters here. Meaning, one's perception of labor and delivery experience is a greater predictor of PTSD than the actual events themselves. Arguably, trauma results from an experience or challenge that we felt unable to meet appropriately ("survive") because of a lack of resources. Obviously, it's a bit more complex than that, but it helps us to understand how our perception shapes our experiences.

Other risk factors for PTSD include a previous trauma (physical, sexual, or emotional), loss of control during labor (unexpected interventions or outcomes), feeling coerced during pregnancy or birth, or have a sense of mental defeat during labor (giving up, feeling overwhelmed, hopeless, or as if you couldn't go on).

Postpartum Psychosis

<u>WARNING: THIS IS A VERY SERIOUS CONDITION REQUIRING HOSPITALIZATION.</u> Postpartum psychosis is very rare. Approximately one to two out of every one thousand women will experience this condition. However, when it does occur, it is extremely serious and all precautions should be taken to address it immediately. Consider this an EMERGENCY situation. The most common symptoms of psychosis are delusions (strange beliefs) and/or hallucinations (hearing/seeing something or someone that is not there) along with confusion and disorientation. This isn't a one-off "did you hear that?" or feeling foggy from the physical exhaustion from birth and taking care of a newborn. **A person who is experiencing psychosis is having a "break with reality" and will struggle to orient themselves in place and time.** It's different than thinking today was Monday instead of Tuesday. High levels of irritability and a decreased need for sleep are also common. Significant mood changes with poor decision-making (risk-taking) along with a "hyperactive" demeanor may also be present. In this case, the treatment protocol is almost always close observation by medical professionals (why hospitalization is required) and medications. Those who do experience an episode can and do recover, but immediate and ongoing help is needed.

BREASTFEEDING & MATERNAL MENTAL HEALTH:
A COMPLICATED RELATIONSHIP

I think it's also important to take note of the ways in which breastfeeding can affect mental health. We know two things: breastfeeding can impact mental health and mental health can impact breastfeeding. Determining which came first— the mental health concern or the breastfeeding concern— is challenging. Studies have shown that breastfeeding can reduce the risk of perinatal mood and anxiety disorders. Meaning, it's protective. Some of this may be from the reduction in the stress hormone cortisol found in breastfeeding mothers. We also see that inflammation levels in the body are lower, something that is believed to be linked to mental health disorders. In addition, some of the hormones present in breastfeeding mothers may be linked to *reduced* sleep deprivation! Meaning, breastfeeding may help a mama get better or more restful sleep, which may help fend off some mental health disorders.

Studies have shown that one of the biggest breastfeeding factors linked to perinatal mood and anxiety disorders is one's breastfeeding intentions. Planning to breastfeed and, for whatever reason, not breastfeeding leads to an increased risk for PMADs. Someone who planned to breastfeed and went on to breastfeed is among the lowest risk group for PMADs. Most studies point to other psychosocial factors that can be somewhat hard to isolate and measure but should be noted nonetheless.

An intention to breastfeed, without going on to breastfeed, leaves many reporting they feel like a failure. There are also many reports about the impact of social pressure on breastfeeding experiences. While we don't have an excellent grasp on these factors at present, we cannot dismiss the impact they have on individual experiences.

Additionally, those who intend to breastfeed and do not are more likely to report pain and exhaustion, which is linked to an increased risk of depression.

Finally, the desire to avoid medications to treat PMADs, fearing breastfeeding will have to cease, should also be noted as influential in this complex relationship.

In most cases, medication can be taken while breastfeeding. See the Resources section for more information.

How does a mother's mental health affect breastfeeding? Studies have indicated that a mother who has a history of anxiety and depression is more likely to report issues with breastfeeding. Interestingly, another study demonstrated that breastfeeding is more likely to decrease the risk of PMADs for someone with a history of trauma and depression than for their counterparts with the same histories who were not breastfeeding. Again, this shows that breastfeeding can be a protective factor for mental health. This nerd finds that so darn fascinating! Those who have been diagnosed with postpartum anxiety are more likely to not initiate breastfeeding, less likely to exclusively breastfeed, and more likely to terminate breastfeeding earlier. Postpartum anxiety can reduce feelings of self-efficacy, which may explain the breastfeeding difficulties.

Here are the takeaways from this primer on the complicated relationship between breastfeeding and perinatal maternal mental health:

1. Support those who want to breastfeed. A good breastfeeding experience can do marvelous things for well-being.

2. Offer compassionate support for those who had intended to breastfeed but do not end up doing so. Quality care can do marvelous things for well-being.

POST-WEANING DEPRESSION

Many are surprised to learn that mamas can experience depression following weaning. It's normal to experience many feelings about ending breastfeeding. Depending on your experiences with breastfeeding and the reasons for ending nursing, feelings of both relief and sadness are quite normal. Endings can bring on feelings of loss. While these feelings are normal, they usually dissipate or lessen after a few weeks. However, in some experiences, these feelings persist or even worsen. Much like birth, hormones are a key suspect in explaining these changes in mood. Prolactin and oxytocin both drop off when no longer lactating. While there is limited research on this subject, some researchers suggest that how rapidly weaning occurs may influence the risk of developing depression. Regardless of the timing of weaning experiences, I believe it's beneficial to explore feelings of loss and sadness (see Chapter 5 on mourning).

TREATMENT

When to Get Help

The severity and persistence of symptoms are key indicators it may be time to seek help. Generally, if symptoms are persisting longer than two weeks and are severe enough to affect the quality of one's day to day life, and if there is a threat of harm to mom, baby, or both, it may be a sign of PMADs and an indication to seek treatment.

There are many different treatment options one may want to consider when addressing a PMAD. For many people, a unique combination of several approaches works well to relieve their symptoms. It's never a one-size-fits-all solution when it comes to mental health and wellness. Some people like to start with the low-intervention options first. All these have been shown to be beneficial in scientific studies. Keep in mind, however, that what works for one might not work for you. Diversify what you're trying and don't give up!

Protect Sleep

The human brain and body need sleep for optimal functioning. No surprise, we're hurting for it postpartum. The idea of protecting sleep is truly the notion of fully appreciating the value (it's not a luxury) and planning accordingly to get the most out of your sleep opportunities. Ideas: Snag some sleep when you can. If you are opting to rest or nap while the baby is, say no to the guest who wants to visit during that time. Resist the urge to mindlessly scroll your phone at bedtime (studies show that the blue light could impact the quality of our sleep). If you're rotating night feedings with your partner, consider sleeping in another room to ensure you're not going to be distruped. I dedicated an entire chapter to sleep, so be sure to revisit the comments there as well.

Nature

Nature therapy is actually a personal favorite of mine, but I'll spare you an entire chapter on the matter. The great outdoors can do wonders for mental and physical health. In fact, the mere presence of nature (view of trees out a window, indoor plants, natural light flowing into a room) can help boost mood and improve overall well-being. The best part is you don't have to go on strenuous or challenging hikes in the mountains or swim in an ocean to benefit. The data shows that simply getting outside for a gentle, wandering stroll or brisk walk (or heck, just getting some sun on a patio) can offer mood-boosting benefits.

Exercise

Exercise can reduce anxiety, depression, and boost your mood. It can also improve cognitive functioning and self-esteem. Interestingly, it's been associated with improving social withdrawal symptoms.

Hydrate

Dehydration can affect energy levels, mood, and the ability to think clearly. A study out of the University of Connecticut reported that women subjects perceived tasks as more difficult when slightly dehydrated.

Improve Nutrition

The medical and scientific community recognizes that diet and mental health are related. In fact, there is an entire field dedicated to this intersection called nutritional psychiatry. Some general guidelines include whole grains and legumes, plenty of fruits and veggies, fatty fish, and healthy fats.

Mindfulness Meditation Practice

Mindfulness and meditation have been demonstrated to be effective at improving sleep, lowering stress, improving attention, and lowering anxiety and depression symptoms. I also mention more about this in the "superpower" chapter and an example is also provided in the Extras section.

Light Therapy

Light therapy can ease the symptoms of depression, specifically seasonal affective disorder (or seasonal depression). Some also report benefits when treating sleep disorders or nighttime shift work, which certainly may be applicable to the postpartum period. Light therapy requires that you sit under (or near) a light therapy box designed to replicate natural outdoor light.

Massage

Massage can lower cortisol (the stress hormone) by an average of thirty percent. As cortisol levels decline, serotonin increases by an average of twenty-five percent. This means a massage (most studies look at a sixty minutes for an average length) can boost the body's ability to cope with anxiety and feelings of sadness.

Acupuncture

Studies have indicated that acupuncture can release endorphins, which can boost mood. Acupuncture has also been demonstrated to be effective at reducing the release of stress hormones by the hypothalamus.

Increase Social Interaction/Support

Isolation can be a breeding ground for anxiety and depression symptoms. I talk about this in greater detail in Part III: Connection. In short, we know that connecting with other humans and socialization (on the whole) is good for our mental health and well-being. Additionally, the data has been extremely consistent on this topic: a healthy social support network is the greatest "medicine" for overcoming challenges and adversity. I call this medicine, "the People Pill." If you are able and have access, reinforcing and growing this network is generally time and energy well-spent.

Consider a Postpartum Doula

A postpartum doula provides various supportive services for families in the days, weeks, and months following the birth of a baby. They are trained and knowledgeable on topics such as emotional and physical recovery from birth, infant feeding, infant soothing, and basic newborn care. A postpartum doula can be extremely valuable in caring for you while you care for your newborn, especially if you don't have family close by or a network of friends to rely on to help get you through those foggy first days.

Laughter

Every Friday I share "Friday Funnies" on my social media pages with the hashtag #laughterismedicine. Laughter, in an oversimplified explanation, can "trick" the brain and boost your mood. Laughter can alter serotonin and dopamine activity, and the endorphins secreted during laughter have been demonstrated to help when you're uncomfortable or depressed. Science aside, learning to laugh at the wackiness of parenting is essential to weathering the storms a bit easier. Making light of our children's shenanigans is also a great means to connect with other parents. This relates to the ideas we talked about when addressing impression management. So get silly!

Cannabidiol (CBD)

CBD is one of nearly two hundred cannabinoids that can be found in marijuana plants. CBD is not psychoactive. At present, studies are limited, but there have been some potential beneficial outcomes noted in the early trial studies regarding anxiety and depression treatment.

Therapeutic Treatments

The next level of intervention involves seeking outside support for most people. This support generally comes in the form of different therapeutic treatments. Much like the "lower level" interventions, you may have to try several of these in different combinations to find what works for you.

- Pharmaceutical medication (i.e. a prescription from a doctor)
- Psychotherapy for yourself or with your partner

All forms of psychotherapy (aka counseling or therapy) have some universal elements. Several theorists and scholars have commented on these, but, in general, most conquer that respect and positive regard, genuineness, warmth, and empathy are essential core components. Meaning, any therapist you work with is trained and experienced in conveying each of these.

In my opinion, the psychotherapy approach a counselor utilizes is less important than the relationship you build with your therapist (known as therapeutic rapport). Finding a therapist that you "click" with is more valuable than whether they use a certain approach. To help you figure out how to find a therapist, I created a brief guide to finding the right fit for you therapist, which you can find in the Extras section of this book.

"I am in the process of becoming the best version of myself."

Unknown

Conclusion

Dear Mama,

I hope you've found some solace in these pages. I hope you've seen yourself in some of the stories I've shared here and that it's made you feel less uncertain and alone. I hope you feel less overwhelmed and perhaps even amazingly equipped for the journey. I hope you feel seen and known. Above all, I hope you feel loved.

I don't know you, but I know that you're doing one of the hardest things any of us can ever do. Raising tiny humans is no joke. It's all consuming. It's exhausting. It's scary. It's wonderful. It's beautiful. It's amazing. It's all of this and more.

I work with so many mamas who ask, after sharing their struggles with me, "Is this normal?" The answer is almost always yes. There may be other hard things that make coping strategies difficult to access, but hard is normal. Hard is universal. When I sit with mamas and hold space for them around their hard stuff, they feel seen and heard. That validation and normalization often goes a long way. There is almost always a subtle (or not-so-subtle) sigh of relief. Then we work from there. We dig into the depths of their personal stuff on top of the baseline hard stuff to find a path to feeling better.

In sharing these thoughts with you, I hope that you too will be able to breathe a sigh of relief in finding that hard is normal. My words here are a simple attempt to get real by challenging our cultural narratives around the transition to parenthood. My expectation is not that these ideas will be the end of your search for understanding, but only the beginning. The parenting journey is a lifelong, ongoing experience, not something that happens as a one-time event. We are forever on a quest—across somewhat uncertain seas—trying to do the best by ourselves, our partners, and our unique children. May you find that the thoughts, tools, and tips within these pages are useful as you navigate these waters and apply beyond this time of transition. I wish you encouragement and love as you forge ahead on your parenting path.

With love,
Amanda

Extras

Tips for Anxiety

Finding a Right Fit Therapist

Loving-Kindness Meditation

ADDITIONAL EXTRAS CAN BE FOUND AND DOWNLOADED AT
WWW.AMANDAHARDYPHD.COM/BOOKEXTRAS

Tips for Anxiety

GROUNDING

Grounding is a lot like what it sounds like. It's the practice of standing exactly where you are in the present moment. Anxiety is like a swirling tornado tossing us around in the strong winds. Grounding is about coming down out of that spiral and standing in the present moment—not the what ifs that anxiety wants us to focus on. One of the most common ways to ground is by activating each of your five senses. Name five things you can see, four things you can touch (I often suggest actually feeling the ground under your feet), three things you can hear, two things you can smell, and one thing you can taste. This exercise can work well even if you don't apply the counts, but some find the counting helpful.

RANK

Ranking your worries means putting them on a scale or giving them a grade. The exercise is based on the notion that if we "file" everything in our brain as a worry we won't be able to tell which ones are actually are worthy of our time and attention to be able to focus on solving them. It's kind of like The Boy Who Cried Wolf, but for our brain.

For this exercise, we create a scale (I like a basic scale from 1 to10). I determine what's a 10 and what's a 1. For me, "10" is a very serious all-alarms-going situation. "1" is a nuisance, a pebble in my shoe, a shoulder shrug situation.

From here, I can get a sense of where other worries may fall. This exercise helps me have a better grasp on what's an 8 versus a 3 and determine how I am going to delegate my energy toward the situation. It doesn't mean I don't care about a 3 or it suddenly doesn't worry me at all. Of course, it does—if it registers on my scale, it means I care. Rather, this helps me say, "This is just a 3. I am not giving it more time and energy than it deserves." Whereas an 8 might demand I stop what I'm doing and address the situation.

This ranking and scale system can also be extremely useful in communicating with our partners. Telling my partner that I'm "worried" or "freaking out" about something might sound all the same. Saying, "this feels like a 9 to me right now" lets them know where I'm really at in my feelings. It helps me remember that I'm in the driver's seat, not anxiety. "This is only a 4, so I'm not giving it 8-level attention." Finally, it's a great way to measure if your coping strategies are working. Something that used to be registering as a 7 is now a 5. Or I was able to assess myself as I came down out of that anxiety tornado—a 9 to a 7 to a 5 and then a 3.

SAY IT OUT LOUD

Anxiety does a really good job of turning these thoughts into taboos. Anxiety convinces us that if we mention what we are thinking, it will come true. If it hides in the dark, somehow we're protected from that scary thing we're thinking. A prime breeding ground for anxiety is fear and shame (things we keep hidden in the dark). Therefore, the truth is anxiety dies when we bring it to light. We need to cultivate safe spaces to speak about our anxious and scary thoughts, such as with a spouse, a parent, a best friend, or a professional. The more you find or create these spaces for yourself and you refuse to listen to the lies anxiety tells you, the less of a hold they will have on you.

These techniques, or any aimed at treating anxiety, aren't about "making anxiety stop." As I've mentioned before, stress and anxiety are naturally occurring states. We actually want these biological response systems working in tip-top shape. What we don't want is overactivated systems—chronic stress or anxiety disorders. The goal of these techniques or any treatment is to help manage anxiety, not eliminate it completely. I like to think of these strategies as taking the edge off. They make that anxiety cliff feel more like a rolling hill. As with anything, practice is the key. Grounding may help the first time to reduce the length of an anxiety episode, but it may have taken a lot of effort. With time and practice, it will become more natural, work faster, and, generally, you'll need it less and less.

Finding a Right Fit Therapist

Having a good rapport with your therapist is essential to the healing relationship. While all therapists are trained in techniques to build this rapport, meet their clients where they're at, and promote comfort, sometimes we don't click. That's okay. Just because a therapist wasn't right for you right now doesn't mean that another might not be a better fit. Here's the catch, few of us have the resources (time and money) to invest in shopping around for a therapist. Therefore, it's helpful to be intentional when you set out to start therapy. Here's a brief list to get you started.

IDENTIFY POSSIBLE OPTIONS

For many people this means looking into their health plan networks to check that a therapist is covered by their insurance provider. What's covered and how much is going to vary—a great deal—by insurance provider. Many therapists are in-network with several providers, but that doesn't always mean that therapy will be covered by a plan. This can feel a bit overwhelming and lots of insurers have member support lines you can call to ask a customer service rep to help you narrow your search. Often you can do this search on a website through your insurer, as well. You can ask about location, accessibility, specialty, and even gender. I suggest identifying 3-5 therapists who meet some of your key criteria.

Psychology Today also provides a directory and verification of license on their website (psychologytoday.com). However, to be listed in the directory therapists have to pay. Therefore, it will not be a comprehensive list, but it's pretty widely used and respected. Many therapists have google or yelp business listings too. Meaning, you don't have to rely on an insurance provider alone to help you generate a good list.

If you do not have health insurance, or no coverage for mental health, be aware that many therapists do accept cash or offer sliding scale fee options.

If you cannot afford to see a therapist, it may still be valuable to reach out to one that you have identified as a potential good fit. Many therapists may be able to direct you to other groups or resources that could still be beneficial.

DO YOUR HOMEWORK

It's helpful to have a general understanding of therapeutic approaches that you might align with. While all therapy includes compassion and empathy the theoretical approach of the therapist will also influence the course of therapy. Here are a few of the common approaches you might want to familiarize yourself with, keeping in mind, a therapist may utilize several of these techniques in conjunction with one another, depending on the client's needs.

- **Cognitive behavioral therapy (CBT):** Works to identify and change patterns of thinking or behavior that may be unhealthy or negative.

- **Dialectical behavior therapy (DBT):** Focuses on behavioral skills aimed at stress and emotional management to improve relationships.

- **Acceptance and commitment therapy (ACT):** Emphasizes increasing awareness and acceptance of thoughts and feelings, and committing to making changes to increase your ability to cope with and adjust to situations.

- **Psychodynamic:** Explores unconscious thoughts and behaviors. Emphasizes the development of insight around internal motivations and drives.

- **Interpersonal:** Addresses interpersonal skills and problems within relationships.

- **Mindfulness-based cognitive therapy (MBCT):** Brings together CBT and mindfulness techniques aimed at helping participants better understand and manage their emotions and thoughts.

- **Eye movement desensitization and reprocessing (EMDR):** Uses bilateral sensory input, such as side-to-side eye movements or hand tapping to work through challenging or distressing experiences. Developed in the 1990s by Francine Shapiro, this approach has been demonstrated to be effective at processing and treating trauma.

CHECK SPECIALIZATIONS, TRAININGS, CERTIFICATIONS, AND LICENSURE

For the most part, therapists are educated and trained to meet a wide variety of mental health needs. However, after schooling many will seek additional training and specialization—in techniques (like EMDR or play therapy) or populations (perinatal or children). You'll want to find out if the therapist you're thinking about seeing has any specific expertise on the issue you're looking to find support for. Often, therapists will list such things on their websites or public directory profiles. If not, you'll want to make sure to ask. Additionally, it may be valuable to find out what type of license they have—temporary or new issue versus full (this may vary by state)—or if they hold certifications related to the specialization.

If you're looking for a specialist in perinatal mental health (as is the subject matter of this book): Postpartum Support International is a good source. They provide an online directory at: www.psidirectory.com.

REACH OUT

Eventually, you're going to have to reach out and make contact with a potential therapist. Check to see if they offer consultation appointments. If they do you may want to take advantage of that low-risk (low-or-free cost) meeting to see if you click. Even if they don't offer consultations, you can often get a good feel for a person via this first contact. You'll want to share a bit about your issue and ask questions that you haven't been able to answer from the "do your homework" section. How you feel about the response you get is a good start to how you might feel about this person in therapy. If it doesn't feel "right," trust your intuition and keep moving on your list.

IT'S OKAY TO MAKE A CHANGE

If you're not feeling it, that's okay. Therapy should feel safe and comfortable and appropriately challenging. While it's not fun to hop around to different therapists, finding someone you can trust is absolutely essential, so don't be afraid to change course.

It can be a big decision to seek therapy and in order for it to be beneficial to you finding that right fit can be monumental. Take your time to research and check in with your feelings about someone and make a change if or when necessary.

Loving-Kindness Meditation

The loving-kindness meditation, also called Metta Sutta, can be traced to ancient India. It is said to pre-date even The Buddha. Studies have shown that expressing kindness and compassion, which is the focus of this meditation, can increase happiness! This meditation promotes connection with others—from close family and loved ones to friends and even strangers. Practicing this meditation can decrease our attention on ourselves, which has been linked to a reduction in anxiety and depression symptoms.

Meditation invites and encourages us to be present in the moment. And that, it would seem, can make us happier. The exciting thing about all this mediation research is that some studies have indicated that in a little as 10-20 mins a day we can reap the benefits of these practices.

This meditation promotes our inherent ability to grow and cultivate kindness. We do this by mentally sending kindness, compassion, and goodwill to yourself and others. This is done by repeating a series of phrases to yourself.

You can find many versions of this meditation by searching online or by downloading phone apps that feature meditations (see Resources). I've provided a script for you to practice this meditation here. Adapt it to fit your needs.

BODY AND BREATH

Sit in a comfortable position. Relax your body. Close your eyes and turn inward as you concentrate and gently repeat the phrases to yourself. Take several slow breaths in and out.

RECEIVE

Think of someone whom you love from your past or present, who is living or not. Imagine this person with you now, sending you love. They send you wishes for happiness and well-being. Receive these wishes of kindness and love.

Think of someone who loves you from your past or present, who is living or not. Imagine this person with you now, sending you love. They send you wishes for health, wellness, and happiness. Receive these wishes of kindness and love.

Imagine yourself surrounded by people you love and who love you.

Think of all your loved ones and friends. Imagine all of them surrounding you. Each one is sending you wishes for your health, happiness, and well-being. Receive these wishes of kindness and love.

As you receive these wishes, feel yourself filled with warmth and love.

SENDING

Think again of the person who you love. Send love to this person as they did for you. Recognize that you and this person are similar—they wish to be happy and well. Send kind and loving wishes to this person. Repeat this mantra to yourself: *May you be happy, may you know peace, may you be loved.*

Think again of the person who loves you. Send love to this person as they did for you. Recognize that you and this person are similar—they wish for a good and happy life. Send kind and loving wishes to this person. Repeat this mantra to yourself: *Just as I wish, may you be happy, may you be safe, may you be healthy.*

Think again of the loved ones and friends. Send love to these people as they did for you. Recognize that you and these people are similar—they wish for happiness. Send kind and loving wishes to this person. Repeat this mantra to yourself: *May your lives be happy, healthy, and satisfying.*

EXPANDING

You may also wish to think of acquaintances or neutral people to send loving-kindness to just as you've done with the others above.

Next, you can expand your thoughts to the entire world and all beings. Send your love and wishes for happiness. Recognize that, like you, they want to be happy.

Just as I wish, may you live a life of happiness, peace, and wellness.

REST AND RETURN

You should take as long as you'd like to imagine yourself sending and receiving love and repeating these phrases.

Rest for a time in the state of mind you've cultivated. Raise your awareness regarding how you're feeling.

Concentrate on your breath. As you feel ready, open your eyes.

Resources

MINDFULNESS & MEDITATION

- *Buddhism for Mothers: A Calm Approach to Caring for Yourself and Your Children* by Sarah Naphtali (2003).

- *Aware: The Science and Practice of Presence — a Complete Guide to the Groundbreaking Wheel of Awareness Meditation Practice* by Daniel J. Siegel (2018).

- *Mindful Motherhood: Practical Tools for Staying Sane During Pregnancy and Your Child's First Year* by Cassandra Vieten (2009).

- *Mindful Moments for Busy Moms: Daily Meditations and Mantras for Greater Calm, Balance, and Joy* by Sarah Rudell Beach (2018).

- The Mindful Mamas Club: www.mindfulmamasclub.com/

- Mindful Mama — My quest to live mindfully: http://mindfulmama.com/

- *The Miracle of Mindfulness* by Thich Nhat Hanh (1975).

- Daring to Rest Academy (www.daringtorest.com) Karen Brody.

- Loving-Kindness Meditation for Moms: www.mindful. org/a-loving-kindness-mediation-for-moms

- Radical Self-Love with Loving-Kindness Meditation (audio): www.mindful.org/this-loving-kindness-meditation-is-a-radical-act-of-love

- Meditation Apps (free and subscription options)
    - Insight Timer
    - Calm
    - Headspace

MAMA-CENTERED PODCASTS

- Mom & Mind

- The Balance & Motherhood

- What Fresh Hell: Laughing in the Face of Motherhood

- The Birth Hour

POSTPARTUM

- *The First Forty Days: The Essential Art of Nourishing the New Mother* by Heng Ou, Amely Greeven, and Marisa Belger (2016).

- *Birth in Four Cultures: A Crosscultural Investigation of Childbirth in Yucatan, Holland, Sweden, and the United States* by Brigitte Jordan and Robbie Davis-Floyd (1993).

- *Zuo Yuezi: An American Mother's Guide to Chinese Postpartum Recovery* by Guang Ming Whitley and Kai Tsu Easlon (2016).

- *What No One Tells You: A Guide to Your Emotions from Pregnancy to Motherhood* by Dr. Alexandra Sacks and Dr. Catherine Birndorf (2019).

- *Strong as a Mother: How to Stay Healthy, Happy, and (Most Importantly) Sane from Pregnancy to Parenthood: The Only Guide to Taking Care of YOU!* by Kate Rope (2018).

- *The Fourth Trimester: A Postpartum Guide to Healing Your Body, Balancing Your Emotions, and Restoring Your Vitality* by Kimberly Ann Johnson (2017).

- *The Postpartum Plan Workbook* by Erin Huiatt (2019).

- *Build Your Nest: A Postpartum Planning Workbook* by Kestrel Gates (2016).

RELATIONSHIPS

- The After Birth Plan Workshop (https://www.doctorberlin.com/the-afterbirth-plan) Dr. Alyssa Berlin.

- *Becoming Us: 8 Steps to Grow a Family that Thrives* by Elly Taylor (2014).

- *To Have and to Hold: Motherhood, Marriage, and the Modern Dilemma* by Molly Millwood (2019).

- *How Not to Hate Your Husband After Kids* by Jancee Dunn (2017).

LACTATION & MEDICATION

- Sources to review if you are concerned about taking medications while breastfeeding or pumping
    - LactMed: www.ncbi.nlm.nih.gov/books/NBK547435 (app available to download)
    - Infant Risk Center at 806-352-2519 (app available to download)
    - MommyMeds: www.mommymeds.com
    - The Lactation Pharmacist: www.thelactationpharmacist.com
    - E-lactancia: www.e-lactancia.org

- Hale's Medications & Mothers' Milk by Dr. Thomas W. Hale PhD (2019).

PERINATAL MOOD & ANXIETY DISORDERS

- Postpartum Support International: postpartum.net
    - Provider Directory: psidirectory.com

- Postpartum Stress Center: postpartumstress.com

- *Good Moms Have Scary Thoughts: A Healing Guide to the Secret Fears of New Mothers* by Karen Kleiman and Molly McIntyre (2019).

- *This Isn't What I Expected: Overcoming Postpartum Depression* by Karen R. Kleiman and Valerie Davis Raskin MD (2013).

- *The Pregnancy and Postpartum Anxiety Workbook: Practical Skills to Help You Overcome Anxiety, Worry, Panic Attacks, Obsessions, and Compulsions* by Pamela S. Wiegartz, Kevin L. Gyoerkoe (2009).

- *Birth Trauma: A Guide for You, Your Friends and Family to Coping with Post-Traumatic Stress Disorder Following Birth* by Kim Thomas (2013)

- *Heal Your Birth Story: Releasing the Unexpected* by Maureen Campion (2015)

- *Daddy Blues: Postnatal Depression and Fatherhood* by Mark Williams (2018).

CHILDBIRTH

- *Pregnancy, Childbirth, and the Newborn: The Complete Guide* by Penny Simkin, Janet Whalley, Ann Keppler, Janelle Durham, and April Bolding (2018).

- *Expecting Better: Why the Conventional Pregnancy Wisdom is Wrong and What You Really Need to Know* by Emily Oster (2013).

- *Ina May's Guide to Childbirth* by Ina May Gaskin (2003).

- *Nurture: A Modern Guide to Pregnancy, Birth, Early Motherhood and Trusting Yourself and Your Body* by Erica Chidi Cohen and Jillian Ditner (2017).

- *Babies Are Not Pizzas: They're Born, Not Delivered* by Rebecca Dekker (2019).
    - Additionally, an online childbirth resource that informs, empowers and inspires expecting parents and birth-care practitioners globally, to understand the latest, proven, evidence based care practices found at www.evidencebasedbirth. com

- *Gentle Birth, Gentle Mothering: A Doctor's Guide to Natural Childbirth and Gentle Early Parenting Choices* by Sarah J. Buckley (2005).

- *Creating Your Birth Plan: The Definitive Guide to a Safe and Empowering Birth* by Marsden Wagner (2006).

- *The Positive Birth Book: A New Approach to Pregnancy, Birth and the Early Weeks* by Milli Hill (2017).

HISTORY OF BIRTH IN AMERICA

- *Lying-in: A History of Childbirth in America* by Richard and Dorothy C Wertz (1977).

- *The Trials of Hanna Porn: The Campaign to Abolish Midwifery in Massachusetts* by Eugene R. Declercq, PhD found at: ajph.aphapublications.org/doi/pdf/10.2105/ AJPH.84.6.1022

- The Campaign to Eliminate the Midwife by Dawley in *American Journal of Nursing* (2000).

- The Official Plan to Eliminate the Midwife from 1900 - 1930 by Faith Gibson, LM, CPM, Community Midwife found at: collegeofmidwives.org/collegeofmidwives.org/ safety_issues01/rosenbl1.htm

- Birth in the United States: An Overview of Trends Past and Present by McCool, WF and Simeone, SA. in *The Nursing Clinics of North America* (2002).

- From Social to Surgical: Historical Perspectives on Perineal Care During Labour and Birth by Dahlen, Homer, Leap and Tracy in *Women Birth* (2011).

References

INTRODUCTION

1. Osho. *The Book of Woman.* India: Penguin Books, 1976.

2. *Harry & Meghan: An African Journey.* Dir. Nathaniel Lippiett. 2019.

BACKGROUND

1. K. B. Kozhimannil, C. M. Trinacty, A. B. Busch, and A. S. Adams. "Racial and ethnic disparities in postpartum depression care among low-income women." *Psychiatric Services* (2011): 619–625.

2. Wagner, Marsden. "Technology in Birth: First Do No Harm." *Midwifery Today,* 2000.

3. Amnesty International. "Deadly Delivery: The maternal health crisis in the US." New York: *Amnesty International, Demand Dignity Campaign,* 2011.

4. Nina Martin and Renee Montagne. "The Last Person You'd Expect to Die in Childbirth." *ProPublica & NPR,* 2017.

5. US Center for Disease Control and Prevention (CDC). 2015. Health United States 2015: With Special Feature on Racial and Ethnic Health Disparities. Atlanta: CDC.

6. Declercq, E R, et al. "Major Survey Findings of Listening to Mothers(SM) III: Pregnancy and Birth: Report of the Third National U.S. Survey of Women's Childbearing Experiences." *The Journal of Perinatal Education* (2014): 1058-1243.

7. Anaïs Nin. *Seduction of the Minotaur.* Chicago, IL: Swallow Press, 1961.

8. Brené Brown. *Rising Strong.* New York: Spiegel & Grau, an imprint of Random House, 2015.

9. Barbara Katz Rothman. "The Social Construction of Birth." *Journal of Nurse-Midwifery* (1977): 9-13.

10. Foucault, Michel. *The Birth of the Clinic: An Archaeology of Medical Perception.* Presses Universitaires de France, 1963.

11. Davis-Floyd, Robbie. "The technocratic, humanistic, and holistic paradigms of childbirth." *International Journal of Gynecology & Obstetrics* (2001): S5-S23.

12. Hardy, Amanda. "The United State of Birth: A Feminist Crique." Iowa State University: Graduate Theses and Dissertations, 2011. www.doi.org/10.31274/etd-180810-1218

PART I

1. Kanes, S. "Brexanolone iv efficacy in postpartum depression in three pivotal trials." *American Journal of Obstetrics & Gynecology,* (2019): S69-S70.

2. Jane Taylor, Editorial Review of *With a Gift for Burning* by Laura Apol, 2018.

3. "The Mother." Track 4 on By The Way, I Forgive You. Low Country Sound / Elektra, 2018. Brandi Carlile.

4. Harvey Karp. *The Happiest Baby on the Block: The New Way to Calm Crying and Help Your Newborn Baby Sleep Longer,* 2015: Bantam Press.

5. Sarah Ockwell-Smith, "The Fourth Trimester – AKA Why Your Newborn Baby is Only Happy in Your Arms." 2012. https://sarahockwell-smith.com/2012/11/04/the-fourth-trimester-aka-why-your-newborn-baby-is-only-happy-in-your-arms/ (accessed October 2019).

6. Kimberly Ann Johnson. *The Fourth Trimester: A Postpartum Guide to Healing Your Body, Balancing Your Emotions and Restoring Your Vitality*, 2017: Boulder, CO, Shambhala.

7. Polan, HJ. and Ward, MJJ. "Role of the mother's touch in failure to thrive: a preliminary investigation." American Academy of Child and Adolescent Psychiatry, 1994:1098-105.

8. RIKEN. "Why do babies calm down when they are carried?." ScienceDaily. www.sciencedaily.com/releases/2013/04/130419160717.htm (accessed October 5, 2019).

9. Molly Millwood. *To Have and to Hold: Motherhood, Marriage, & the Modern Dilemma*, Chicago: Harper Wave, 2019.

10. Dana Raphael. Being female: reproduction, power, and change. The Hague: Mouton, 1973.

11. 2018. "A new way to think about the transition to motherhood." May 2018 in New York. TED video, 6:08, www.ted.com/talks/alexandra_sacks_a_new_way_to_think_about_the_transition_to_motherhood

12. Alexandra Sacks and Catherine Birndorf. *What No One Tells You: A Guide to Your Emotions from Pregnancy to Motherhood*, New York: Simon & Schuster, 2019.

13. Erik Erikson. *Childhood and Society.* New York: W. W. Norton & Company, 1963.

14. Dean Jackson. *The Poetry of Oneness: Illuminating Awareness of the True Self.* South Carolina: Createspace Independent Publishing, 2013.

15. Douglas J. Blackiston, Elena Silva Casey, and Martha R. Weiss. "Retention of Memory through Metamorphosis: Can a Moth Remember What It Learned As a Caterpillar?" PLOS ONE, 2008. www.doi.org/10.1371/journal.pone.0001736

16. Lewis Carroll. *Alice's Adventures in Wonderland.* Stuttgart, Germany: Macmillan Publishers, 1865.

17. Elisabeth Kübler-Ross. *On Death and Dying.* New York, New York: Simon & Schuster, 1969.

18. Jalāl al-Dīn Rūmī and Barks, Coleman (contributor). *The Essential Rumi.* San Francisco, CA: Harper Collins, 1996.

19. Nakita Valerio. 2019. "Shouting 'self-care' at people…" Facebook, March, 2019.

20. Brianna Wiest. "This Is What 'Self-Care' REALLY Means, Because It's Not All Salt Baths And Chocolate Cake." *Thought Catalog.* Last modified January 14, 2020. https://thoughtcatalog. com/brianna-wiest/2017/11/this-is-what-self-care-really-means-because-its-not-all-salt-baths-and-chocolate-cake/

21. Saundra Dalton-Smith. *Sacred Rest.* Nashville, TN: Thomas Nelson, 2017.

22. Karen Brody. *Daring to Rest.* Louisville, CO: Sounds True, 2017.

23. Siegel, Daniel J. *Aware: The Science and Practice of Presence—The Groundbreaking Meditation Practice.* New York: Tarcher Perigee, 2018.

24. Zlatan Krizan and G. Hisler. "Sleepy anger: Sleep restriction amplifies angry feelings." Journal of Experimental Psychology: 2019, 1239-1250. www.doi.org/10.1037/xge0000522

25. A. Lawson, K.E. Murphy, E. Sloan, E. Uleryk, and A. Dalfen. The relationship between sleep and postpartum mental disorders: A systematic review. *Journal of Affect Disorders,* 2015 (176), 65-77. www.doi.org/10.1016/j.jad.2015.01.017

26. J. Sacher, A. A. Wilson, S. Houle, P. Rusjan, S. Hassan, P. M. Bloomfield, and J. H. Meyer, J. H. "Elevated brain monoamine oxidase A binding in the early postpartum period." *Archives of General Psychiatry,* 2010: 468-474. www.doi.org/10.1001/archgenpsychiatry.2010.32

27. C. E. Schiller, S. Meltzer-Brody, and D. R. Rubinow. "The role of reproductive hormones in postpartum depression." *CNS spectrums,* 2015: 48-59. www.doi.org/10.1017/S1092852914000480

28. J. G. Buckwalter, F. Z. Stanczyk, C.A. McCleary, B.W. Bluestein, D. K. Buckwalter K. P. Rankin, L. Chang, T. M. Goodwin. "Pregnancy, the postpartum, and steroid hormones: effects on cognition and mood." *Psychoneuroendocrinology,* 1999:69-84.

29. M. W. O'Hara, J. A. Schlechte, D. A. Lewis, M. W. Varner.
     "Controlled prospective study of postpartum mood disorders:
     psychological, environmental, and hormonal variables." *Journal
     of Abnormal Psychology*, 1991: 63-73.

30. Robin Edelstein, Britney M. Wardecker, William J. Chopik,
     Amy C. Moors, Emily L. Shipman, and Natalie J. Lin.
     "Prenatal hormones in first-time expectant parents: Longitudinal
     changes and within-couple correlations" *American Journal of
     Human Biology*, 2014. www.doi.org/10.1002/ajhb.22670

31. Ilanit Gordon, Orna Zagoory-Sharon, James F. Leckman, and
     Ruth Feldman. "Prolactin, Oxytocin, and the development
     of paternal behavior across the first six months of fatherhood"
     Hormones and Behavior, 2011: 513–518. www.doi.org/10.1016/
     j.yhbeh.2010.04.007

32. F. Hashemian, F. Shafigh, and E. Roohi. "Regulatory role of
     prolactin in paternal behavior in male parents: A narrative
     review." *Journal of Postgraduate Medicine*, 2016: 182–187.
     www.doi.org/10.4103/0022-3859.186389

33. Kanes, S. "Brexanolone iv efficacy in postpartum depression in
     three pivotal trials." *American Journal of Obstetrics & Gynecology*,
     (2019): S69-S70.

PART II

1.   Elizabeth Kasujja. "The Psychology Behind Never Feeling
     Good Enough." Medium. Accessed Sept. 2019 at www.medium.
     com/swlh/the-psychology-behind-never-feeling-good-enough-
     2ad963d16119

2.   Pauline R. Clance and Suzanne A. Imes. "The imposter
     phenomenon in high achieving women: Dynamics and
     therapeutic intervention." *Psychotherapy: Theory, Research & Practice*,
     1978 (15), 241-247.

3.   Frances Cannon. *Self Love Club*. Self-published zine, 2017.

4.   Carly Snyder. Quoted in "Having a baby is beautiful, but
     postpartum emotions are so hard." *Mashable*, 2015. Accessed
     August 2019 at https://mashable.com/2015/10/25/postpartum-
     emotions-moms/

5. Donald Woods Winnicott. *Playing and Reality.* Chatham, Kent: Tavistock Publications, 1971.

6. Gavin De Becker. *The Gift of Fear.* Dell, 1997.

7. Glennon Doyle. "By the Power Vested in me by Tish: I Declare Today International Do Your Hard Thing Day." Blog. *Momastery.* Published April 4, 2014.

8. Brené Brown. *Rising Strong.* New York: Spiegel & Grau, an imprint of Random House, 2015.

9. Kaitlyn Neath (@MadLibMom). 2018. "Me: I'm tired Women everywhere: Just enjoy the time with your kids. It doesn't last! Me: I said I'm tired, not that I hate my children, Janet. I'm allowed to fucking feel things. #kids #parenting #children #momlife #tired #TuesdayThoughts #bedtime #BabyGirl #babies" Twitter, May 22, 2018. https://twitter.com/KaitlynNeath/status/999090579295297537?s=20

10. Anna Quindlen. *Rise and Shine.* New York, NY: Random House, 2006.

11. Vironika Tugaleva. *The Shades of Missing You.* Soulux Press, 2019.

12. Jean Piaget. *Origins of intelligence in the child.* London: Routledge & Kegan Paul, 1936.

13. Lori Goetlieb. *Maybe You Should Talk to Someone.* Boston, MA: Houghton Mifflin Harcourt, 2019.

14. Ernest Kurtz and Katherine Ketcham. *The Spirituality of Imperfection: Storytelling and the Search for Meaning.* New York: NY, Bantam, 2009.

15. Thomas Merton. *Exploring Solitude and Freedom- The Journal of Thomas Merton.* San Francisco, CA: Harper, 1997.

16. William and Martha Sears. *The Attachment Parenting Book.* New York, NY: Little, Brown Spark, 2001.

17. John Bowlby and Mary Salter Ainsworth. *Attachment and loss.* Vol. I. London: Hogarth, 1969.

18. "Love is All You Need." Single. Olympic Sound Studios, London; EMI Studios, London, 1967. The Beatles.

19. Frank L. Baum. *The Wizard of Oz*. Hollywood, Calif.: Metro Goldwyn Mayer, 1939.

PART III

1. Margaret J. Wheatley. *Turning to One Another: Simple Conversations to Restore Hope to the Future*. San Francisco, CA: Berrett-Koehler Publisher, 2009.

2. Linda Buzzell in *Ecotherapy: Healing with Nature in Mind* (Linda Buzzell & Craig Chalquist, Editors). San Francisco, CA: Sierra Club Books, 2009.

3. Herbert Hoover. *Campaign Speech*, 1928. Website. Digital History Archives. Accessed September 2019 at www.digitalhistory. uh.edu/disp_textbook.cfm?smtID=3&psid=1334

4. Malcolm Gladwell. *Outliers: The Story of Success*. Boston, MA: Little, Brown and Company, 2008.

5. Larry Eubanks. "The Myth of the Rugged Individual." Website: Ethics Daily, published 2014. Accessed September 2019 at https://ethicsdaily.com/the-myth-of-the-rugged-individual-cms-22301

6. Arielle Alden-Danforth. "It takes a village—to raise a mother." Blog: Mother.ly, accessed at www.mother.ly/life/it-takes-a-villageto-raise-a-mother

7. Eider Ruiz-Mirazo, Maite Lopez-Yarto, Sarah D. McDonald. "Group Prenatal Care Versus Individual Prenatal Care: A Systematic Review and Meta-Analyses." *Journal of Obstetrics and Gynaecology of Canada*, 2012(3): 223–229. www.doi.org/10.1016/S1701-2163(16)35182-9

8. Louis Cozolino. *The Neuroscience of Human Relationships: Attachment and the Developing Social Brain*. New York, NY: Norton Professional Books, 2014.

9. Ellen Hendriksen. *How to Be Yourself: Quiet Your Inner Critic and Rise Above Social Anxiety*. New York, NY: St. Martin's Press, 2018.

10. Michael Rosen and Helen Oxenbury (illustrator). *Going on a Bear Hunt*. New York, NY: Alladin Paperbacks, 1989.

11. Steve Flowers. *The Mindful Path Through Shyness. How Mindfulness and Compassion Can Help Free You from Social Anxiety, Fear, and Avoidance.* Oakland, CA: New Harbinger Publications, 2009.

12. Jarrid Wilson. *Love Is Oxygen: How God Can Give You Life and Change Your World.* Colorado Springs, Colorado: NavPress, 2017.

13. Lisa Robinson. "Cover Story: Adele, Queen of Hearts." *Vanity Fair.* Published: October 31, 2016 in print and online December 2016. Accessed at www.vanityfair.com/culture/2016/10/adele-cover-story

14. Taylor Jenkins Reid. *The Seven Husbands of Evelyn Hugo: A Novel.* New York, NY: Atria Books, 2017.

15. Jen Sincero. *You Are a Badass: How to Stop Doubting Your Greatness and Start Living an Awesome Life.* Philadelphia, PA: Running Press, 2013

16. Sensei Ogui. *Zen Shin Talks.* Cleveland, OH: Zen Shin Buddhist Publications, 1998.

17. Jancee Dunn. *How Not to Hate Your Husband After Kids.* Boston, MA: Little, Brown and Company, 2018.

18. Olivia Remes, Carol Brayne, Rianne van der Linde, and Louise Lafortune. "A systematic review of reviews on the prevalence of anxiety disorders in adult populations." *Brain and Behavior.* First published: June 5, 2016 www.doi.org/10.1002/brb3.497

19. Stress in America: Coping with Change. *American Psychological Association.* Report. 2017. Accessed at www.apa.org/news/press/releases/stress/2016/coping-with-change.pdf

20. Carlene Boucher. "A Qualitative Study of the Impact of Emotional Labour on Health Managers." *The Qualitative Report,* 2016: 2148-2160. Accessed at https://nsuworks.nova.edu/tqr/vol21/iss11/15

21. Jennifer Garcia-Alonso, Matt Krentz, Deborah Lovich, Stuart Quickenden, and Frances Brooks Taplett. "Lightening the Mental Load That Holds Women Back." Website: Boston Consulting Group, published: April 10, 2019. Accessed at www.bcg.com/publications/2019/lightening-mental-load-holds-women-back.aspx

22. Aliya Hamid Rao. "Even Breadwinning Wives Don't Get Equality at Home." The Atlantic, Published: May 12, 2019. Accessed August 2019 at www.theatlantic.com/family/archive/2019/05/breadwinning-wives-gender-inequality/589237

23. Rebecca M. Horne, Matthew D. Johnson, Nancy L. Galambos, and Harvey J. Krahn. "Time, Money, or Gender? Predictors of the Division of Household Labour Across Life Stages." *Sex Roles*, 2018 (78): 731–743. www.doi.org/10.1007/s11199-017-0832-1

PART IV

1. Judy Dippel, *Breaking the Grip of Postpartum Depression.* Independently published, 2017.

2. NIH: Task Force on Research Specific to Pregnant Women and Lactating Women (PRGLAC). 2019. *Recommendations on Perinatal Mood and Anxiety Disorders (PMAD) in Pregnant and Lactating Women.* Eunice Kennedy Shriver National Institute of Child Health and Human Development (NICHD).

3. Kathleen Kendall-Tackett. "Four Research Findings That Will Change What We Think About Perinatal Depression." *Journal of Perinatal Education.* 2010: 19(4), 7–9. www.doi.org/10.1624/105812410X530875

4. C.T. Beck. "Post-traumatic stress disorder due to childbirth: the aftermath." *Nursing Research,* 2004: 53(4), 216-24.

5. M.W. O'Hara and J. E. McCabe. "Postpartum depression: current status and future directions." *Annual Review of Clinical Psychology:* 2013(9), 379-407. www.doi.org/10.1146/annurev-clinpsy-050212-185612

6. Christine H. Ou and Wendy A. Hall. "Anger in the context of postnatal depression: An integrative review." Birth, 2018; www.doi.org/10.1111/birt.12356

7. A. F. Bell, C. S. Carter, J. M. Davis, J. Golding, O. Adejumo, M. Pyra, and L. H. Rubin. Childbirth and symptoms of postpartum depression and anxiety: a prospective birth cohort study. *Archives of Women's Mental Health,* 2016: 19(2), 219-227.

8. Karen Klieman and Molly McIntyre. *Good Moms Have Scary Thoughts: A Healing Guide to the Secret Fears of New Mothers.* Familius, 2019.

9. P. O'Brien, Karen Anthony, A. McNeil, Richard Fletcher, Agatha Conrad, Amanda J. Wilson, Donovan Jones, and Sally W Chan. "New Fathers' Perinatal Depression and Anxiety— Treatment Options: An Integrative Review." *American Journal of Men's Health,* 2017: 863–876.

10. Borra, C., Iacovou, M., & Sevilla, A. (2015). New evidence on breastfeeding and postpartum depression: the importance of understanding women's intentions. *Maternal and Child Health Journal,* 19(4), 897-907.

11. Clemson, C., Meltzer-Brody, S., Colquhoun, H., Riesenberg, R., Epperson, C. N., Deligiannidis, and Kanes, S. Brexanolone iv efficacy in postpartum depression in three pivotal trials. *American Journal of Obstetrics & Gynecology,* 2019: 220(1), S69-S70.

12. Gavin, N. I., Gaynes, B. N., Lohr, K. N., Meltzer-Brody, S., Gartlehner, G., & Swinson, T. (2005). Perinatal depression: a systematic review of prevalence and incidence. *Obstetrics & Gynecology,* 106(5), 1071-1083.

13. Goodman, J. H. (2009). Women's attitudes, preferences, and perceived barriers to treatment for perinatal depression. *Birth,* 36(1), 60-69.

14. O'Hara MW, Schlechte JA, Lewis DA, Varner MW. 1991. Controlled prospective study of postpartum mood disorders: psychological, environmental, and hormonal variables. *Journal of Abnormal Psychology,* 100(1):63-73.

15. Paul, I. M., Downs, D. S., Schaefer, E. W., Beiler, J. S., & Weisman, C. S. (2013). Postpartum anxiety and maternal-infant health outcomes. *Pediatrics,* 131(4), e1218-e1224.

16. Pope, C. J., & Mazmanian, D. Breastfeeding and postpartum depression: an overview and methodological recommendations for future research. *Depression research and treatment,* 2016.

17. Tahirkheli, N. N., Cherry, A. S., Tackett, A. P., McCaffree, M. A., & Gillaspy, S. R. (2014). Postpartum depression on the

neonatal intensive care unit: current perspectives. *International Journal of Women's Health*, 6, 975–987. www.doi.org/10.2147/IJWH.S54666

18. Elizabeth Stone. *A Boy I Once Knew*. Chapel Hill, NC: Algonquin Books, 2002.

Acknowledgements

Books are not written in a day, nor are they written in isolation. At least, not for me. This is a passion project. It's been a project in the works since my dissertation was defended in 2011. When I would tell people what my dissertation was about (a feminist ethnography about the history of birth in America), I was consistently asked for a copy. Naturally, I'd warn folks that while it's an interesting topic, it's still an academic piece of research and not "entertaining" to read, while flattered by the requests. I've been told, "you should write a book" for years, and I've always aspired to such. In short, it's taken me years to get to sharing these pages with you. I would not be able to passionately share this work with you, if not for the people who helped me along the way. I would like to take a moment to acknowledge them—for whom I'm truly and deeply grateful.

To the ones who put me on the path to motherhood, Jack and Charlie. Thank you for making me a mama. Thank you for letting me write and not giving me too much flack about all the times you didn't have clean underwear because

I was living a dream in the pages of this book. Thanks for the giggles and snuggle sessions in the "big bedroom" and all the ridiculous arguments about who gets to sleep next to mom. You're my favorite (you know which one).

To my parents. Good lord, I'm so lucky to be your offspring. Great DNA. Highly recommend. You're the absolute best! You know damn well, because you tell me, that I couldn't do this without you. But, the truth is, I wouldn't want to. I love our village, and I'm so grateful for all the ways you love me and my tiny humans. Thanks for keeping me humble by reminding me that I'm still the same pain in the ass I've always been. From the depths of my soul, thank you!

To my sister, Paige. I love how much I learn from being your sister. I love watching you be a mother—all the highs and lows and everything in between. In so many ways, this book is a love letter to you. Watching you on your journey made me want to write this book more than ever, and I hope I did right by you. Thanks for being difficult to love at times—if it was always easy, I don't think it would be as good. Hey, remember that time I biffed it in the lobby of the hotel in Paris? Good times.

To Jenn. I cannot tell you how honored I am to call you friend. I love co-creating awesome badass shit with you and how energizing that campfire magic feels when we're up to something! Thanks for helping me learn how to take care of my curls (geez, what would I do without you). And for letting me talk through every damn step of this book process with you and for every TMI conversation we've ever had. Thanks for being my chosen family. Most of all, thanks for always letting me tag along even when I don't read the itinerary!

To the committee, Courtney, Jen, Brenda, and Emily. Y'all are just the greatest and I love sharing all the TMI details with you. You're a safe haven from the storms and my most favorite mom friends. Thanks for keeping it real—in good times and bad. Thanks for letting me just show up just as I am and loving me anyway. I know my days are better because I get to share them with you (even when quite prolific). Courtney, extra love for your editorial brilliance! This book is better because of you.

To Jeni and Hannah, you've both always loved me in the midst of my messiness, and I can't imagine who I'd be without that acceptance. Thank you for being the kinds of friends who never miss a beat, who I can always come back to, and appreciating me as I am.

To Dallas. I am so glad we were introduced. You were the perfect person to partner with on this project, and I'm grateful for your guidance throughout the process.

To Holly. You are one talented lady. I'm grateful for your many talents, your humor, and your knowledge in working through the process of polishing up this text. You came along at just the right moment and gave me all the energy I needed to cross the finish line.

To those who have come before me. Sir Isaac Newton is cited as having said, "If I have seen further, it is because I stand on the shoulders of giants." This sentiment feels quite appropriate as I reflect on all the brilliant words spoken and published prior to the ones within this book. I am encouraged and influenced by many researchers, activists, mamas, and other all-around badasses. I owe a debt of gratitude to each for their work.

There are so many others who have influenced me throughout the course or who have served as great sounding boards along the way who I sincerely appreciate. Sarah and Karen, my office mates. Kasey and Cosette, who both helped me build my practice by sharing your spaces. Kari, Jessica, and Rebecca awesome midwifery trio and beloved confidants. The doulas, childbirth educators, and lactations support in my community (Emily, Melissa, Katie, Jenny, Kelli, Erin, Angela, and so many others) thank you for loving on these families in all the ways you do, you are an inspiration every day! Every colleague who has chatted with me in the copy room about matters relating to mamas (Megan, Amie, Meghan, Diana, Laura, Christine, Jenn, and Ji-Young). Sedahlia and Cathy, thanks for reading that dissertation over and over again, much appreciated! Tracie, my therapist, thanks for listening to all my bullshit! The mamas who were willing to read this content before I made it public, your reassurance that it was worthy is priceless.

To every client who I've ever had the pleasure of being on a journey with. From my doula clients to my therapy clients. Thank you for your trust and your willingness to welcome me into the most intimate and intense moments of your life. I am forever honored and grateful for the experiences we've shared. Each of you has taught me about life and love, and I offer my deepest and most heartfelt gratitude. An extra special thank you to those of you who have allowed me to share details of your stories within these pages.

About the Author

On her oldest son's first birthday Amanda Hardy took her first class as a PhD student in Human Development and Family Studies at Iowa State University. Prior to this, Amanda had earned a master's degree in psychological counselling from Monmouth University in West Long Branch, New Jersey and had worked in the mental health profession for several years. In 2008, when her first child was born, she was working as a therapist at a residential facility for children, many of whom had experienced significant trauma in their lives.

Amanda's own experiences with her pregnancy and birth along with her work with these clients ignited a curiosity about the link between attachment patterns and our birth experiences. Upon re-entry into graduate school and the need to establish a research agenda, Amanda began to explore questions about childbirth, child development, parenting, and the ways in which these three interact and intersect.

Her dissertation study was a qualitative inquiry exploring American women's experiences in childbirth. Both feminist and historical perspectives were used during the study. Her study aimed to address the questions "how did we get here (maternity care crisis) and what does it mean for moms, babies, and families?" There was no shortage of women willing to share their stories for this study. Amanda completed that work and successfully defended her dissertation in 2011 (while in the first trimester of her second pregnancy).

Since completing her PhD Amanda hasn't stopped talking to families about their birth experiences. Over the past decade she has volunteered for and served in a leadership capacity with several nonprofits aimed at addressing issues in our maternity care system and supporting families (most notably Improving Birth). In fact, she even founded a non-profit (now dissolved) with the goal of increasing access to evidence-based care across her home state of Iowa. As a result of these experiences Amanda has heard thousands of birth stories from people all over the world.

She is a faculty member at Iowa State University and has also worked as a doula and childbirth educator. In 2017, Amanda opened a small part-time private practice in her community offering mental health support for perinatal mood and anxiety disorders. And much like her experience with her dissertation research, there was no shortage of people who needed to talk about their birth and parenting journeys. In early 2019, Amanda was the second person in Iowa to earn her certification in perinatal mental health through the non-profit organization Postpartum Support International.

Amanda is a self-professed wanderlust and is always plotting her next adventure. Camping and backpacking are her personal favorites. She lives in Iowa with her two sons and a village of extended family and friends.

Visit *https://amandahardyphd.com* to learn more.

Printed in Great Britain
by Amazon